CW00467631

return to mounta.

tai chi

Also by Dolores LaChapelle

Earth Festivals

Earth Wisdom
(English & German editions)

Sacred Land, Sacred Sex, Rapture of the Deep:
Concerning Deep Ecology and Celebrating Life
(English & German editions)

Deep Powder Snow
(English & Italian editions)

D.H. Lawrence: Future Primitive

Also by John Marshall

A Simpler Way (with Dan Mesich)

Living (and dying) In Avalanche Country (with Jerry Roberts)

Mining the Hard Rock (with Zeke Zanoni)

return to mountain

between heaven and earth

DOLORES LaCHAPELLE

PHOTOGRAPHY JOHN MARSHALL

Photo by Danielle

John Marshall, Christchurch,
New Zealand, 2002

Copyright © 2002 Dolores LaChapelle
Photographs copyright © 2002 John Marshall

First published 2002

The author has asserted her moral rights in the work.

This book is copyright. Except for the purposes of fair reviewing,
no part of this publication (whether it be in any eBook, digital,
electronic or traditionally printed format or otherwise) may be reproduced
or transmitted in any form or by any means, electronic, digital or mechanical,
including CD, DVD, eBook, PDF format, photocopying, recording,
or any information storage and retrieval system, including by any means
via the internet or World Wide Web, or by any means yet undiscovered,
without permission in writing from the publisher.
Infringers of copyright render themselves liable to prosecution.

ISBN 1-877270-30-X

Hazard Press is an imprint of Hazard Publishing Ltd

Published by Hazard Publishing Limited
P.O. Box 2151, Christchurch, New Zealand
Telephone: +64-3-377 0370
Facsimile: +64-3-377 0390
email: info@hazard.co.nz
www.hazardonline.com

Seasonal calligraphy by Chungliang Al Huang

Printed in China by Everbest Printing Co.

Contents

Preface

I've been pondering on the events that led to this book for twenty-six years, ever since I began Tai Chi and discovered the incredible interactions with nature which this discipline provides. But first, I must explain how it came about that I have lived in mountains all my adult life.

Each winter for sixteen years I lived in the Ski Resort of Alta, Utah, where my husband Ed, did snow and avalanche research for the U.S. Forest Service. We had one son, David. We lived in the Ranger Station and rode a rope tow to get up to our cabin. I taught skiing and home-schooled my son and the other three children dwelling in our valley. Each summer we lived up on the Snowdome in the middle of the Olympic Mountains in Washington where Ed was in charge of the Blue Glacier study project. The project began with the International Geophysical Year in 1956. Of course no one had ever lived up there before, but a building was constructed and research instruments flown in and we spent each summer high up on the Snowdome. In spring and fall we lived in Kirkland, Washington and Ed taught at the University of Washington.

We were back in Alta for the winter of 1970. That year marked the beginning of the planning stage for the big new resort, Snowbird. Ed knew this would mean no research time for him as there would be too much avalanche control work each day. Two options turned up for him.

Ed got the contract for snow research on the effect of cloud seeding on avalanches so in 1973 we would be moving to Silverton high in the San Juan Mountains.

Meanwhile, the 1972 Olympics were scheduled for Sapporo, Japan. Ed had been asked to join the snow scientists at the Japanese Cold Weather Institute there in Sapporo for the winter.

Although these were interesting mountain projects I was devastated at the thought of leaving the perfect Alta powder snow. Nowhere in the world is there such good powder. I thought, "I'll die without powder snow."

Meanwhile, that summer was again spent on the Blue Glacier in the Olympic

Peninsula. Toward the end of summer, friends from Utah had hiked the 20 miles into the Snowdome to visit us and I walked out with them as we came off the glacier. I took them to the "last wild beach in conterminous United States", a remote beach on the Olympic Peninsula. While there, my two friends began moving in this strange, flowing manner. I was watching from the top of a nearby rock. When they finished I asked "What was that?" They replied: "Our version of Tai Chi." And I knew my life was saved. I could sense the same flowing movement with no effort that real powder skiing provides.

After another winter in Alta we returned to Kirkland in the spring of 1971 and I found a teacher, Raymond Chung, who came down once a week from Vancouver, Canada, to teach Tai Chi. I was able to complete only the first of the three sections of Tai Chi before we went back to the Blue Glacier for the summer. As soon as I got everything organized in the hut for cooking and cleaning and getting water from melting snow I headed up to Panic Peak to do Tai Chi. This is a small rock "nunatak" left by the scouring of the glacier long ago. On one side it drops right off to the Pacific Ocean five thousand feet below; on the other side we see Mt. Rainier and the mountains of Vancouver Island in Canada. I scraped the gravelly rocks away to make a flat place just below the summit and began the slow, circling movements of Tai Chi. When I finished I was amazed. I had seen a mountain I had never seen before! Now, you must realize that I had been walking up to the summit and sitting on it and looking, looking for something like sixteen years. I had watched sunrises and sunsets and storms and thought I knew every mountain. And now I saw a new mountain I'd never seen! I realized that Tai Chi certainly helps one see better. I began using

Panic Peak on the Olympic Peninsula in the State of Washington.
Photo by Joe Stock

it as a "seeing" tool for figuring out climbing routes and even, when in the city, for viewing art shows in Seattle.

I got a few more lesssons in Tai Chi in the fall before we left for Sapporo, Japan in November 1971. In Japan I continued doing Tai Chi every day. Fortunately in Sapporo one can see the nearby mountains. Doing Tai Chi and watching the mountains move, I found, gave me a very grounded at-home feeling within a few days, even though I never actually went into those mountains to ski until some time later.

During the Winter Olympics there were special exhibits for all the "foreigners" and I was immersed in the aesthetics of Japan. Such events are held on the top floors of the big department stores. When I saw that a Tea Ceremony was scheduled, I took the elevator up to the top floor. I got off the elevator and walked through an arch and was suddenly immersed in gorgeous fall birches. I found myself automatically moving Tai Chi style. It affected me deeply. Of course when I stopped to figure it out, I saw the corridor went between two walls of vastly enlarged color slides - 6 ft. tall and back-lit so that one was engulfed in the color and light of fall. I had never seen photographs so skillfully used to create a close relationship between human and nature.

We subscribed to the *Japan Times*, an English language newspaper published by the Japanese. Sometime after the Tea Ceremony event I read a startling account concerning a famous photographer, Kira Sugiyama and his model. There was a one-man show of his work on the eleventh floor of the Odakyu Department Store in Shinjuku. The show was devoted to the nude photos of his most famous model, Yaeko Ota. It turns out that he discovered her when she was seventeen and had been photographing her for five years. He spoke of her "vibrant beauty and her purity" and had "extolled her virginity." But she had fallen in love meanwhile and, although she knew that the photographer did not know about her affair, she "apparently felt that she had betrayed the trust of Sugiyama" and she committed suicide.

There is a particular genre of photographs in Japan called "nymph gamboling in beautiful scenery," which comes out of a very ancient concept of the *miko*, the sacred maiden who dances for the *kami* (god) in the important Shinto shrines.

The photos accompanying the article showed Ota with flowers or under trees but the photos were so obviously posed that they lost any innate relationship with nature around her. I thought that if a young woman did Tai Chi outside, the flowing movement is not posed so is not false and therefore she would move more naturally within all of nature. This human action would draw the viewer deeper into the beauty of nature; thus it would inspire action to preserve the natural environment.

We returned to the United States in March of 1972 and moved to Silverton for the avalanche project. I continued doing Tai Chi in the midst of the wild San Juan Mountains and soon discovered the effect of Tai Chi on wild animals. I already knew that house cats will come right into the center of a group doing Tai Chi to soak up the energy and that dogs will lie down close by and never move until the Tai Chi ends. I had not expected this to happen with wild animals but it did. The most incredible encounter concerns a pine marten.

Often I climb a 12,900 ft. mountain called Golden Horn because it's a perfect place to do Tai Chi. The route is up a narrow rock ridge but just below the summit there is a flat platform which a glacier carved out of the narrow ridge. It's just big enough for two people and absolutely flat but the view is out over dozens of steep vertical mountains on every side.

This particular time a friend and I had climbed to the top and then come down to this platform to do Tai Chi. As we did the form, birds were chirping on every side. This is most unusual at such an altitude. As we completed the 108 forms, we both felt something over our shoulder. Turning, we looked directly into the eyes of a pine marten with its glorious tail waving above it in the wind. He just sat there watching us. Then, I assume, because he no longer felt any more of that Tai Chi energy, he turned and disappeared among the rocks on his way down. Suddenly, we realized why there had been so many bird calls. He had climbed up the buttress from tree line, robbing nests on the way and those were alarm calls. Pine martens don't live that high.

I've lived in areas where there are pine martens for years and never seen one before. They are not prone to be near humans at all. This one deliberately came to see what we were doing, because he "felt" something different than the usual energy that humans put out. There's no other explanation for a pine marten to be sitting watching you until you turn around and even then, stay comfortably sitting there gazing at you.

In 1976 I wrote my first book, *Earth Festivals*. After it was published, I was invited to Claremont, California to meet with Arne Naess, Paul Shepard, Joe Meeker, and others to begin the New Natural Philosophy program. Arne, who began the Deep Ecology movement, came over from Norway for the meeting. My second book, *Earth Wisdom*, was published under this program. A year later the New Natural Philosophy Program was disbanded. In 1980 there was an Earthday X Colloquium. George Sessions and I both gave papers concerning Deep Ecology, thus beginning the Deep Ecology movement in this country. I continued my work for the environment by writing articles and giving workshops and lectures at various colleges; but my most important work was giving Tai Chi lessons at workshops held outside by rivers or on mountains. I spent three years writing *Sacred Land, Sacred Sex, Rapture of the Deep: Concerning Deep Ecology and Celebrating Life*. It was published in 1988 and praised as the first and only complete manual on experiential deep ecology. My book *Deep Powder Snow* was published in 1992, followed in 1996 by *D. H. Lawrence: Future Primitive*. During all this time I remained hopeful about the Tai Chi project.

Finally, two years ago here in my own town of Silverton under fortuitous circumstances I found a photographer and the young woman for Tai Chi and felt that I could put the book together that I had envisioned for the last 25 years. Jodi Harper-Nute easily learned Tai Chi from me becasue she was a gymnast. She has a degree in Biological Aspects of Conservation from the University of Wisconsin so she felt deeply for nature in all its aspects. Fortunately, the photographer, John Marshall, had done a book titled *Living (and dying) in Avalanche Country*, which showed the full drama of intense personal encounters with nature at its wildest. But most important, both John and Jodi were deeply tied to our San Juan Mountains and could feel and express their love for our mountains. Out of the thousands of photos we took through each of the four seasons, we chose the ones which showed the particular Tai Chi form which best brought together the essence of that place within that particular season. The photos manifest our attempt to capture the exquisite nature of that combination. Within a short time we began to register in our bodies how this connection felt.

Jodi's flowing movements in Tai Chi begin to pull you more deeply into your own place We purposely chose to photograph always within 15 minutes of a road or highway in our San Juan County - to show that one doesn't need to invade the wilderness to feel the deep beauty of nature both without and within. Deep inside, we humans are still natural and that registers for us within the old brain located in the lower abdomen, where the chi energy dwells.

With all the media propaganda about the new millennium it's important to remember that it's just a paper calendar which originated in the Roman Empire era and has nothing to do with real human life in this year and nothing to do with nature around us either. Tai Chi master Al Huang tells us that this year is the Chinese Earth-Hare year of 4697. Gary Snyder points out that we've been the same human for at least 40,000 years. For all that time we've been doing art - going back to the cave art in the Dordogne and the Pyrenees – Snyder says: "We can hear their language coming through paintings of lions and bison." This language expresses itself in poetry and story telling and chanting and moving deeply from the old brain, the tan tien. Shamans danced from that center and Tai Chi forms still do. All of these are the "old ways", temporarily interrupted by 400 years of the Industrial Growth Society. In reality, Gary Snyder says, our "*homo sapiens calendar*" begins about 40,000 years ago. We can reclaim our true nature any time by living deeply, living fully in our own place. This book helps you remember how.

The 108 Forms of
TAI CHI CH'UAN

Section One

1.   Commencement of T'ai Chi Ch'uan
2.   Grasp Bird's Tail (right style)
3.   Grasp Bird's Tail (left style)
4.   Ward Off Slantingly Upward
5.   Pull Back
6.   Press Forward
7.   Push
8.   Single Whip
9.   Raise Hands and Step Up
10.   Stork Spreads its Wings (1st Part)
11.   Stork Spreads its Wings (2nd Part)
12.   Play the Fiddle
13.   Brush Knee and Twist Step (1st)
14.   Brush Knee and Twist Step (2nd)
15.   Brush Knee and Twist Step (3rd)
16.   Play the Fiddle
17.   Brush Knee and Twist Step (L)
18.   Chop Opponent with Fist
19.   Step Up, Deflect Downward, Parry and Punch
20.   Apparent Close Up
21.   Embrace Tiger, Return to Mountain

Section Two

22.   Ward Off Slantingly Upward, Pull Back, Press Forward and Push
23.   Diagonal Single Whip
24.   Fist Under Elbow
25.   Step Back and Repulse Monkey (R)
26.   Step Back and Repulse Monkey (L)
27.   Step Back and Repulse Monkey (R)
28.   Step Back and Repulse Monkey (L)
29.   Step Back and Repulse Monkey (R)
30.   Slanting Flying
31.   Raise Hands and Step Up
32.   Stork Spreads its Wings
33.   Brush Knee and Twist Step (L and R)

Tai Chi

This brief introduction to Tai Chi is designed not only to give you some basic concepts but also an insight into the thousands of years involved in the heritage of Tai Chi. The real learning for you comes as you go through the book and experience Jodi doing Tai Chi with the mountains.

The name, Tai Chi comes from the ancient Chinese classic, *I Ching*. It refers to the Pole Star, which remains stationary while all the constellations revolve around it. The Chinese felt that not only the entire natural universe revolved around this Polar Star but also human culture as well. In fact the same word, Tai Chi, was used for the ridge-pole of human houses. An early description of the philosophical depth of this concept was made by Chou Tun-I (1017–l073). From the turning of the Tai Chi, also translated as the Supreme Ultimate, comes the yin and the yang. The movement continues in the Yin direction but then it always turns around and moves the other way toward the Yang. Out of this action comes the five elements of China: water, fire, wood, metal and earth. These five elements "diffuse harmoniously, and the Four Seasons proceed on their course." Later, due to Taoist influences, the famous Sung dynasty philosopher Chu Hsi developed the concept further. This on-going process is not due to any one thing producing all the rest. Instead there is a continual, moving, interrelated action of all these elements. Because this essential concept is difficult to grasp I will go deeper into it before continuing with this introduction to Tai Chi.

The European tradition of science has always searched for the ultimate substance, leading to the idea of atoms and ever smaller distinct bits of matter, while the Chinese tradition sees reality as relationship. This is partly due to language structure. European languages must have a subject, something that does the action. The Chinese language does not have this construction. Locked into the narrow confines of subject in our culture, a thing is either one thing or the other – good or bad. In Chinese thought, first of all since there is no subject, there is no 'thing.' Second, there is no locking into one identity, therefore no permanent classification such as good or bad or any other dichotomy. Rather, Chinese thought emphasizes the relationship quality between above and below, good and evil, something and nothing. In Taoist thought it is called "nothingness or no-particular-thing-ness."

Obviously, we are getting deeply into language traps here so I will return to mountains to clarify "no-particular-thing-ness." When walking up a trail in the valley you see each individual peak rising up above the trees. As you begin climbing out of the valley, you suddenly find more mountains rising up behind the first mountains you saw. You continue climbing until you are at the top. There, you suddenly discover that all those individual mountains were actually part of the one mountain. They were outlying peaks - joined by ridges all culminating in the summit you are standing on. Are there a number of different things or one thing?

From the Chinese point of view it is seen and recognized that each is a different manifestation of the whole and changing all the time as well. We can see that the Western world's concentrating on substance is similar to a person seeing a particular mountain peak from the main valley and studying each peak separately and accumulating massive amounts of data without ever having glimpsed the fact that each of these little peaks is part of the whole main mountain massif. The Chinese, with their underlying concept of relationship, were able to discern that it's all connected together and furthermore, that everything is always changing.

The West is beginning to move out of the substance trap due to the work of Gregory Bateson on the nature of mind, which led to new scientific approaches in Western thinking. Bateson's premise is that the mental world, the mind - the world of information processing - is not limited to our skin. The system which we ordinarily call "self" does not have a boundary which ends with the skin. The information coming to this self includes all the external pathways along which information travels such as other human minds, light, sound, temperature, and all aspects of earth and sky. Bateson explains:"essentially your ecosystem, your organism plus environment, is to be considered as a single circuit...and you are *part* of the bigger circuit." The arbitrary lines we draw between human and the environment are purely artificial, fictitious lines. They are lines drawn "*across* the pathways along which information or difference is transmitted. They are not boundaries of the thinking system. What thinks is the total system which engages in trial and error, which is man plus environment." Bateson's work was crucial for the development of systems theory and the newer sciences growing out of it such as chaos theory, organismic biology, and dissipative structures. These relatively new sciences bring a realization of the interrelationships inherent in all of nature. Finally, after hundreds of years, we are rediscovering what the Chinese Taoist inspired science knew long ago. However, our culture, in general, is still caught in the substance trap. Rational thinking won't get us out of it. But Tai Chi can help. Now to return to the Pole Star.

While doing Tai Chi, the person's own backbone is the mountain aligned with the Pole Star, around which the body continually turns one way or the other in spiral, circular motions.

Tai Chi developed over thousands of years from three main sources. One was the shamanic practices of northern Asia, which included "animal frolics". For example, the Shaman would dance the bear to cure kidney problems. The second source was Southern, extending as far as the Polynesian cultures. The third and later influence came from the Buddhist conversions in China. The actual forms we still use today in Tai Chi reflect these ancient developments. "Step Up to Form Seven Stars" is based on the ritual dance of the Great Yu, legendary emperor of the Hsia dynasty (2000 to 1520 BC), symbolizing "the intercourse between Heaven (yang) and earth (yin). Another example concerns the form, "Wave Hands Like Clouds". A stone engraving on an ancient tomb shows a woman doing precisely the same form we use today. This engraving was found on an on an early Tang Dynasty (618 to 906) tomb, excavated in 1973-4.

Tai Chi has developed into many different styles through the centuries. One of the main sources came from the monastery in the Shaolin mountains, dating back to the time of the Buddhist, Bodhidharma. He arrived in 475 in Canton and his teaching developed into Chan Buddhism in China and Zen in Japan.

Wen-Shan Huang, in his book *Fundamentals of Tai Chi Chuan*, calls Chang San-Feng the founder of Tai Chi Chuan. He was appointed District Magistrate of Chung Shan. He often visited Taoists in the nearby mountains. Eventually, he built a cottage in the mountain of Wu Tang, where he studied the Tao and "finally attained the supreme achievement of creating the art known as Tai Chi Chuan." At one time he spent ten years at the Shaolin Monastery mastering their techniques. Chang San-Feng's contribution was that he taught the importance of the "art of inhalation and exhalation" and "intrinsic energy" which has to do with chi energy. As a Confucianist-Taoist, he emphasized the breathing system which had been practiced in China increasingly since the days of Chuang Tzu (369–286 BC). Chang San-Feng lived in the latter part of the Northern Sung dynasty (960-1279).

I will not go further into the complex story of the later developments of Tai Chi. Most important was the Chen clan and later, the Yang family. Most of the Tai Chi taught in the U.S. today is based on the Yang form which was originated by Yang Lu-Ch'an (1799-1872).

Both of the main divisions of Tai Chi began in the mountains.

1) Southern School, the soft form, originated at Wu Tang Mountain. Later developments were such groups as Pa Kua in China and Judo and Aikido in Japan.

2) Northern School, the firm or hard form, originated in the Shaolin mountains.

In the course of this book you will see Tai Chi in our wild San Juan Mountains of Southern Colorado. But first, as is the custom, I must give the lineage of my teachers. Fortunately, I began studying Tai Chi in 1971 before it became popular in this country. Tai Chi first attracted widespread attention in this country in 1972 when President Nixon went to China to discuss trade agreements. During random shots of Chinese life, the TV cameras showed hundreds of people doing Tai Chi outside in the park. In the next few years it became obvious to Chinese martial arts practitioners that there was a market for their services in this country. The arrival of such random teachers ultimately produced a general confusion of the forms.

My teachers lived in Vancouver, Canada, so they had many years of careful attention to the forms. Both of my teachers had the famous portrait of Chang San-Feng on the wall. My first teacher was Raymond Chung, who came down to Seattle from Vancouver once a week. In the spring of 1971 I began studying with him. In the fall we went to Japan as my husband was asked to do avalanche research with the Japanese Cold Weather Institute. I had only learned part of the entire 108 forms from Chung. When we got back from Japan in the spring of 1972, I found that he had decided he would no longer come to the U.S.

My second teacher was Master Tchoung Ta Tchen who had been an officer in the Chinese Nationalist army years ago. He was sent up in November to investigate the defenses on Mt. Omei, one of the Buddhist sacred mountains in China. He was dressed in a modern heavy army overcoat and winter gear. When he arrived at the top he found a small man, lightly dressed and with bare feet sitting on a rock. He did not interrupt the man's meditation but was so curious he came up again the next day and they talked. My Sifu (the honorary Chinese title for teacher) said he wanted to learn from this man so the small man, as a test, said, "Follow me." Barefoot, he ran over fields of boulders. Sifu could not follow. That's when he began studying Tai Chi.

Sifu had to leave China because he was a Nationalist and either the Japanese or the Communists would be taking over soon. He spent decades in South Africa before moving to Vancouver. In the early 1970s. he came down once a week to Seattle's Chinatown to teach. Winters my husband and I lived in Silverton, studying avalanches, but I studied with Sifu from spring through fall from 1973 to 1976. From him I learned the double Tai Chi form and began learning Tai Chi Jyan (Tai Chi sword) before I began living in Silverton all year round.

My Sifu was 67 years old when I began studying with him. He had not a grey hair on his head and his face was totally unlined. Most interesting of all, in the mid-1970s he returned to China to visit his teacher, who was then over 100 years old. He was one of the "immortals" as they call them in Taoism.

I experienced such a sense of the the power of Chi Energy from classes with Master Tchoung Ta Tchen, that I determined to pass it on to others. After moving to Silverton full time I began teaching Tai Chi at Fort Lewis College in Durango and in 1976 I began teaching here in Silverton. I have taught every year since then. I also teach certain key Tai Chi forms as part of the mountain workshops and Deep Ecology workshops I give throughout the Western United States.

Seasonal Wheel of the Year

"Heaven and earth and the natural seasons 'move' according to a prescribed order, and according to this 'movement,' new phenomena or 'root-traces' are born."

Ansho Togawa

Changing relationships between the yin and the yang and all the powers of the our four directions interact in the San Juan Mountains to bring about this "movement". Following Jodi's movements of Tai chi through the seasons, you become aware of the "root-traces" both in nature and in yourself.

Fundamentally, the changing relationship between the sky and the earth throughout the year produce the patterns (Chinese, *li*), which we, here on earth, call the seasons. The solstices and the equinoxes are the four prominent alignments of sun and earth: each of these is the beginning of one of the four seasons. At the Spring Equinox the equatorial plane of the earth is in direct line with the sun which makes day and night of equal length. During the winter the North Pole has been tilted away from the sun but with the Spring Equinox it again begins tilting in toward the sun. Thus the sun's rays shine more directly on the northern hemisphere and we get warmer weather. By the time of the Summer Solstice the sun has reached its northernmost setting point on the horizon. On that day it spends the longest time visible in the sky during the year. The following day it begins its journey back along the horizon to its winter setting point. Again at Autumn Equinox we have equal day and night and the beginning of autumn. When the sun reaches its farthest setting point on the southern horizon we have the shortest day of the year. This is Winter Solstice and the beginning of winter. The word solstice comes from two Latin words: *solstitium* meaning *sol*, sun, and *sistere*, "to stand still." Although the sun doesn't really stand still it seems that it does because one day it's approaching this point, the following day it sets right on this point and the third day it's moved back so little that it is not noticeable without some obvious landmark.

As mentioned before, the origins of Tai Chi were connected with Taoism. The famous Taoist, Chuang Tzu, tells a wonderful story of the dry empty skull along the roadside. Everyone literally sleeps each night pillowed on his skull so this story is about relationships not only within oneself and within nature but between human and nature. Chuang Tzu says this about the skull: "With the heaven and earth it makes rounds of spring and autumn." Kaung Ming Wu, in his book about Chuang Tzu, writes that this phrase is "casually tossed out by the dry roadside skull to describe its 'ineffable joy.' " "The heaven and earth" is nature:"spring and autumn" is the round of seasons. "With nature to make seasons is to let nature roll in season after season, to let all spaces be at all times, to roll space and time into one -- in short, to let things be as they are. This is joy unperturbed through ups and downs, season and after season."

It's the reciprocal appropriation of all beings of the earth and sky which allow nature to proceed naturally. Chuang Tzu's second chapter concerns the mutual pipings of human, earth and heaven. In "piping", Kuang Ming Wu explains: "The sound comes out from only a vacant hollow or cavity, which is powerless in itself to release sound unless exposed to the wind...neither the hollow nor the wind *alone* is capable of sound; only their mutuality sounds forth." Going deeper: "Nature initiates the self-fulfillment of the nature of each entity which takes what it wants for itself, thanks to Nature." In Chuang Tzu, "the words, the reader, and the message all three appropriate one another." That is reciprocal appropriation.

Reciprocal Appropriation

Reciprocal appropriation is the best phrase I have found for true human/ nature relationship. It is used not only by the Chinese but by at least one famous Western philosopher and also by American Indian thinkers.

Martin Heidegger is the European philosopher who best understood the relationship of human/nature because of his close ties to his own place, Todtnauberg, in the mountains of the Black Forest region of Southern Germany. He states that the human world is produced by the mutual action of the "Fourfold." The earth, the sky, the gods and the mortals of a particular place create the culture of that place. Heidegger uses the German word, *ereignen* , which means the "joint process by which the four of the fourfold are able, first, to come out into the light and clearing of truth, and thus each to exist in its own truthful way, and secondly, to exist in appropriation of and to each other, belonging together in the round dance of their being." The translator, Albert Hofstadter, states that it is because of "this interpenetrating association of coming out into the open, the clearing, the light – or disclosure – with the conjunction and compliancy of mutual appropriation, that I have ventured to translate "das Ereignis" as "the disclosure of appropriation."

Anthropologist Keith Basso, in his lifelong study of the Western Apache, *Wisdom Sits in Places* (1996), states: "A number of other American Indian authors, among them Vine Deloria (Standing Rock Sioux), Simon Ortiz (Acoma), Joy Harjo (Creek) and the cultural anthropologist, Alfonso Ortiz (San Juan Pueblo) have written with skill and insight about the moral dimensions of Native American conceptions of the land. No one, however, has addressed the subject with greater sensitivity than N. Scott Momaday (Kiowa). The following passages, taken from his short essay titled "Native American Attitudes to the Environment" (1976), shows clearly what is involved not only for the Western Apache but for other tribes as well. Basso quotes Momaday: "The native American ethic with respect to the physical world is a matter of reciprocal appropriation: appropriations in which man invests himself in the landscape, and at the same time incorporates the landscape into his own most fundamental experience."

Recently this concept of reciprocal appropriation has become more generally recognized. In a recent issue of the British environmental journal, *Resurgence*, Jerry Mander writes: "The machine is adapted for humans and humans are adapted to the machine. It is a human-machine merger" and shows how "our acceptance of the entire industrial experiment has been a mistake, whether viewed from the social or ecological perspective." In the final paragraph of his article he states: "The first step is to gain consciousness, and to stop engaging in the process which is killing us and killing the planet… . Then we need to…apply such principles and practices as express a reciprocal relationship with nature."

Today, this ongoing reciprocal appropriation of human/nature is being rapidly destroyed and ruptured by world-wide exploitation. Modern technology is domesticating the entire earth and turning humans into mere "consumers" and all of nature into "resources." Lynn Margulis is the famous microbiologist, who co-authored the Gaia hypothesis with Lovelock.

Incidentally, she tells the interviewer, Jonathan White, "I never say the earth is a single live organism. Lovelock might, but not me... . The earth is an ecosystem, or the sum of many ecosystems." She goes into detail about the mutual interrelations on many levels of life on earth and sums it up brilliantly when she says, "Ultimately, it's the quality of life for humankind and other large animals that we affect most profoundly by our behavior. I don't think we should feel embarrassed or ashamed to show concern for our own survival. The earth will live on until the sun dies – it's just a question of whether we'll be a part of its future." It's obvious that we humans must become more aware of the reciprocal appropriation of nature and humans during each moment of our lives here on earth.

Here in our San Juan Mountains Jodi "incorporates the landscape into her own most fundamental experience" while doing Tai Chi through the seasons as she takes part in the "ineffable joy" of the reciprocal appropriation of all beings in our mountains.

冬

Winter

The yin and yang of Chinese thought comes from the changing relationships between the sun and the mountain. In the old form of the Chinese characters *yang* is represented by the sun with its rays, together with the character *fu* , meaning hill or mountain. The character for *yin* was a coiled cloud along with the character *fu*. According to the definition in the *Erh Ya*, a dictionary of the Chou period, yang described "the sunny side of the mountain" and yin, "the side in the shadow." This relates directly to the changing relationship of the sun and the mountain. In the morning, when the sun is behind the mountain, the trees are dark – almost black; in the afternoon, when the setting sun shines directly on these same trees, they are bright and glowing with light.

In this way the yin and yang annually meet each other in the north at the winter solstice, when the yin is dominant and the yang subordinate, and again in the south at the summer solstice, when the reverse is true. They are annually opposite each other at the spring equinox, when the yang is in the east and the yin in the west, and again at the autumn equinox, when their positions are reversed; on both occasions they are exactly equal in length. All this, constitutes 'the course of Heaven', [which] when it has been completed, begins again.

Tung Chung-shu (179-104 B.C.)

In Jodi's movement you can feel the dance of the sky with the earth in the ever changing movement through the seasons. In winter the falling snow floats onto the earth from the sky and she breathes in the vapor from the new fallen snow back out into the sky with every breath.

The trees are dark, because the sun is behind the mountain in this winter morning scene – almost totally yin. But you can see bits of blue sky through the trees and the white old snow below, indicating the beginnings of the movement back toward the brightness of yang.

Form 1 – In this beginning move of Tai Chi, Commencement of Tai Chi Ch'uan, one turns over the arms to "something other" to raise them. I tell my class to think of a puppet master up there with strings attached to your hands to raise them. Arms lift slowly until they are horizontal. The fingers are totally loose and hanging. The chi energy starts from the tan tien in the lower abdomen. You can feel it expand as it moves up through the chest and shoulders and moves out through the fingertips. Then the arms are lowered, palms facing out and new chi energy moves back into the body.

Commencement of Tai Chi Ch'uan

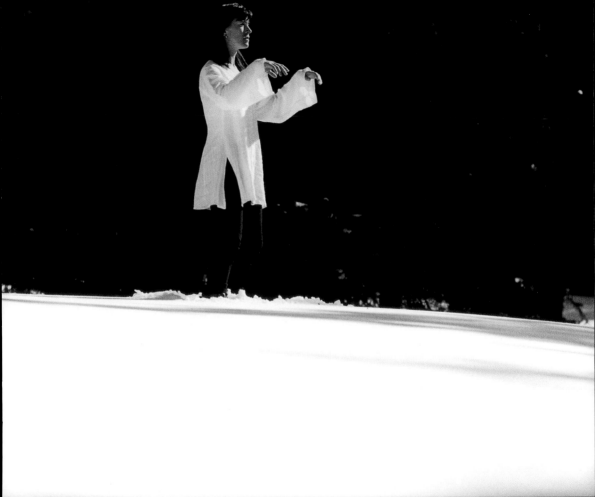

Snow opens its arms and gives away silence.

Robert MacLean

Tai Chi forms follow along with nature. In this form, Jodi's hands cleave to the natural lines. Her left hand mirrors the flatness of the fallen snow and her right, lower hand follows the curvature of the snow beginning to cascade over the ice. Her yielding feet in the soft snow add to the chi energy of the moving hands. She lets her world be – in stillness.

Jodi's movements follow Chuang Tzu's "way". "He does not indulge in a blind worship of Nature or a cult of naturalness, but proposes a sensitive non-interference, a transparent resonance with things, a matching of the inner heaven with the outer. Instead…*we* ourselves must enter an evocative resonance among things, by means of which we become ourselves."

Kuang-Ming Wu

Form 2 – The ancient Chinese origin of Grasp Bird's Tail relates to calming a wild bird or a rooster in the old ritualistic cock fights. One hand reaches from below, palm inward, to hold the bird's neck, the other hand moves down to smooth the bird's tail.

> *The aesthetics of fresh snow making the world new again, every morning.*
>
> Lito Tejada-Flores

After completing the earlier forms, Jodi does Single Whip and finds herself effortlessly facing the other way and seeing her Shadow, there before her, when it had previously been behind her. The relationship between Shadow and Jodi is one of reciprocal appropriation. Without her and the snow there is no Shadow; but, in turn, Shadow delineates her form and adds importance to it, allowing the movement, Single Whip to stand out. Chuang Tzu explains this reciprocity of Shadow in his second chapter, titled: "On the Equal Self-Arrangement Among Things."

Reciprocal appropriation also occurs as the white, soft, yielding snow, under the influence of the yang sun of the day becomes, with the yin of night, frozen, drop by drop as it moves down in response to gravity, becoming transparent, hard blue icicles.

Jodi, moving with exquisite balance through the soft, still yielding snow, her Shadow flowing over the snow, the blue ice growing downward – all this ongoing "self-arrangement *among* things indicates that such arrangement obtains in their mutual interaction, to the extent of interdependence and interchanging of identities. These two qualities – distinct identities (*yu fen*) obtained in their interchanges (*wu hua*) – make up the world." Kuang Ming Wu continues by pointing out that these two important phrases conclude Chuang Tzu's Chapter Two and appear often in his later chapters.

Form 8 – Single Whip, is used throughout Tai Chi to change direction. Here, Jodi has completed form No. 7, Push, while facing the rock. Turning on her right heel, her body forms a right angle to her hips. Then, making the hook with her hand she steps out facing the other direction, with the rock behind her.

Single Whip

Jodi continues moving through the snow, the fingers of her left hand mirroring the icicles. Her right hand, palm down, interacts with the flat snow with the earth beneath, yin. In Brush Knee Twist Step, one hand brushes the knee as she steps out, then that foot is turned out, rotating on the heel and the hand turns up toward yang, the sky. Then the other foot steps forward, turning out on the heel and the hand turns up. Heaven and earth in each movement as the hands change from yin to yang.

Forms 13 to 15, Brush Knee Twist Step, provide excellent examples of the use of tendon power. The foot turns out after each step, alternately winding and stretching the tendons. The hand moves in a circular motion and then parallel to the earth, moves alongside the ear and then pushes out using the wrist tendon. In Tai Chi the tendons, which are flexible and elastic, are used more than muscles in order to generate chi energy, and provide rooting to the ground as well as power to move with minimum effort.

Brush knee
Twist Step

> *"We never tire of one another – the mountain and I.*
> *Li Po (701–762)*

Jodi greets the "greater power," Grand Turk, her arm and hand automatically mirroring the slope of the mountain and her legs and hands and body turning left and then right around the mountain within her spine. There is a "constant path of effortlessness" as she turns around the axis of her spinal column, where the tiny openings of the vertebrae move the chi energy up and down with each turning out of her foot and turning up of her hand. She follows along with nature and, as Kuang-Ming Wu says: "We feel our way through the invisible vital spinal artery of the energy that pervades the inner self and the entire cosmos."

Our San Juan Mountains were carved out by glaciers during the Pleistocene era. Grand Turk's awesome face was scoured out by the grinding, plucking action of tons of ice with gravity moving the glacier as it slid by the massive rock on its way downhill. In the 1870's the miners named this impressive mountain Grand Turk (13,087 ft.), supposedly because the top resembles a turban. Turk guards the southern boundary of our level valley of Silverton.

In the reciprocal appropriation of sky and earth each winter, the uplift of our mountains causes the snow to drop out of the moisture laden clouds coming in from the storm track across the Pacific. Meteorologists call this "orographic lift".

Form 17, This Brush Knee Twist Step leads into the closing moves of Section I of Tai Chi. The legs are not used to turn; instead the spine is the pivot around which the body turns. The central line of gravity runs from the crown of the head, down through the tan tien, and through the "Gushing Spring" acupuncture point on the soles of the feet and on down into the ground.

Brush knee
Twist Step

" Great One!
Standing and reaching as high as the heavens.
Truly as high as the heavens
In the midst of the paths of the coming winds.
In the midst of the winds you sit...
Ho! This is the desire of your little ones
That we may take part in your strength
Venerable One! "
Omaha Tribal Chant

Jodi begins the concluding move for Section One of Tai Chi. She opens her arms to embrace all the chi energy which has gathered around her. Her arms curve downward and in toward the tan tien and, cupping her hands, she scoops up all the chi energy, lifting it to the heart level. Al Chung-liang Huang calls this Embrace Tiger, Return to Mountain. Tiger refers to chi energy.

Facing the Great Power, Sultan Mountain, Jodi embraces it as part of the on-going interchange of energy in our valley.

Sultan (13,368 ft. high) is a powerful presence for all of us living here in Silverton. After a fierce winter blizzard, when the sun comes out and this great, glorious mountain comes forth from the clouds, each of us, walking down the street, is in awe of its power and beauty.

High on Sultan is a glacial cirque, carved out by the glacier which plucked rocks from above and carried them along frozen in the sole (bottom) of the glacier. These blocks are used by the glacier to scour out the hollow cirque. Now, winter snows and avalanches are held within this huge bowl, so deep that the last of the snow does not melt until early September, thus providing a reserve of snow to keep the streams running and flowing into the Animas: giving life to the fish, water for our town, and irrigation and water supplies for towns clear down into New Mexico. Reciprocal appropriation! Sultan was named by the miners way back in the mining era of the 1870's because they, too, felt its power.

Form 21, The form, Embrace Tiger, Return to Mountain, marks the conclusion of each of the three sections of Tai Chi. The stretching of both arms provides an intense gathering of chi energy - both inhalation and exhalation – into the tan tien. "Movement and stillness become one."

Spring

Spring equinox marks the day when the sun's path crosses the earth's equator from the south toward the north. The word "equinox" comes from the Latin word meaning "equal night". Night and day are the same length. Both the dark side (yin) and the lighted side (yang) of the earth become equal in area from pole to pole during the equinox. The north pole, which has been tilted away from the sun during winter, gradually begins tilting in toward the sun after the equinox so that the sun's rays fall more directly onto the northern hemisphere and the weather begins to get warmer day by day. In the southern hemisphere we have just the opposite. It's true that on spring equinox dark and light are equal but the south pole now begins to tilt away from the sun and so it becomes gradually colder in such places as Australia and New Zealand.

Bad weather can occur around the time of the spring equinox but the general feeling is one of joy: "The sun advancing, the disk rising each day to the north of where it leaped from yesterday and setting north of yesterday's setting, the solar disk burning, burning, consuming winter in fire." The Hopi say that the sun is heading toward his "Summer House".

Here in the San Juan mountains in the month of March when the spring equinox occurs, we still have snow on the ground but on the south sides of the houses in town and the south sides of the rocks and cliffs up on the mountain the snow is melted and often, the bravest of wild plants, the heart leaf buttercup and the erigeron, are beginning to grow. While this is our early spring, the full flowering of spring does not occur here until June.

> *Ice and water, their differences resolved, are friends again.*
> *Traditional Haiku*

Jodi's left hand pushing against the right opens her chest up, allowing her to inhale fully the negative ions created by the falling water, as the spring sun releases the water from the ice.

The southern exposure of the rock holds the heat even after the sun goes down, thus allowing more melt and the power of the water grows. Falling water crashing over the rock liberates negative ions. Negative ions have a calming, healing effect on humans and all mammals. Positive ions produce "ill winds": the foehn of Austria, the chinook of the northern Rocky Mountains, the sirocco of Italy, the mistral of Southern France. The famous painter Van Gogh was particularly sensitive to "bad ions". He cut his ear off during one mistral wind and later committed suicide during another.

When the water molecules are split by hitting the rock, ionization occurs. It becomes a positive ion if one or more electrons are missing; it becomes a negative ion if it has one or more extra electrons. Near waterfalls, there are more of the larger, negative ions while positive ions, being lighter, drift off. Negative ions are also more prevalent around high mountains and in forests and other thick vegetation areas.

Form 6 – Press Forward, opens the body. The lungs expand and the back muscles are strengthened.

> *Cascades of blue ice, glittering light,*
> *Sunlight advances, water trickles down*
> *Spring will blossom,*
> *And the seasons continue to "move".*

Jodi allows her body to push her hands out, thus drawing in chi through the tips of her fingers and her palms. As her body moves her hands out, the chi energy is drawn deeply into her body. All the while she is breathing the healing negative ions from the waterfall.

Waterfalls and high mountains, where negative ions accumulate, are considered "sacred" in many primitive cultures. In modern times the negative ions produced by waterfalls are recognized as healing agents. These effects have to do with serotonin, a brain transmitter and mood-altering substance. High amounts of positive ions lead to what is called "serotonin irritation syndrome" which causes the typical symptoms of what Swiss and Austrians call "foehn psychosis". This results in such symptoms as headaches, irritability, general anxiety, insomnia, nausea, apathy, depression and congestion in the respiratory tract.

Research has shown the "regenerating, invigorating, preventative and curative effect of negative ions." If a change in these microscopic air ions can cause such effects on the human mind, can we still consider the mind to be limited only to what is inside our skull? No, according to Gregory Bateson, who states that the mind, the mental world – the world of information processing – includes the external pathways along which information travels such as light, sound, temperature and all aspects of the natural world – on the earth and under the sky where you dwell. In ancient China it was said that humans result from the interactions of heaven and earth.

Form 7, Push is the fourth movement of the Ward-off, Pull-back, Press-forward, and Push series. This series occurs often throughout the 108 moves of Tai Chi. In the Push form, the body draws the hands gradually backwards until they are near the chest. Then the body moves the two hands out to the push position with fingers upward. The legs and arms are strengthened and the lungs expanded.

> *...stir like icicles on a spring morning & start to dance too, melting steadily, most sweetly & gently...*
>
> Robert MacLean

Jodi shows the rooted balance which Tai Chi provides as she "Steps Up", moving with sure balance on the wet rock midst the melting ice. It is not a precarious balance but a flowing interaction between her and the rock and gravity. The sureness of movement in Tai Chi comes from the interaction between the *tan tien*, the brain, located four fingers below the navel, and the older (so-called reptile) and limbic (animal) brains in the skull.

The rooted balance of Tai Chi that we seek comes from a similar physiological source as that of the Balinese. "A large part of Balinese behavior is based upon the paradigms of balance and the interaction between the moving human body and the gravitational field in which it must move." Gregory Bateson further explains that this "kinesthetic socialization prepares the individual for a temporary escape" from limited rational hemisphere thinking.

For the human, balance is not as simple as it is for our animal relatives with their four legs. If a human thinks too much while moving, the innate balance is upset. For instance, in skiing, too much rational hemisphere control invariably leads to a fall. Tai Chi, in turning movement over to the older brains, taps into our natural animal balance in relation to gravity. The Chinese word for balance translates as "heaven at peace."

Due to their "deeper than rational" balanced interaction with all of nature on their island, the Balinese people have successfully managed to retain their culture even though there are condos and tourists just down the beach from them.

Form 9 – Raise Hands And Step Up, strengthens the spinal column, thus permitting a freer flow of chi energy through the spinal channels.

Raise Hands and Step Up

> *The land speaks to us.*
> *A transliteration of heave, swell and shifting plates.*
> *...and we become fluid.*
>
> *Judyth Hill*

In Stork Spreads Its Wings, Jodi opens her arms slowly and widely just as the stork does, circulating chi energy throughout her body.

My teacher told us this legend about Chang San-feng, the founder of Tai Chi. He was looking out the window and saw a snake hissing up at a stork in the tree. The stork flew down and attacked the snake with its sharp beak. The snake slid away and then lashed at the stork with its tail. The fight continued but when one attacked, the other yielded and the attack didn't work. Eventually, tired of fighting, the crane flew away and the snake slithered back into its hole. Chang San-Feng remembered the Taoist story of how, although water is the weakest element, it can eventually wear down rocks. He realized the importance of yielding and thus developed Tai Chi out of Shao-lin martial arts.

Because our San Juan Mountains are so heavily glaciated, the lower slopes are very steep so there are few flat places. Through the years I have searched for such places – trying to find flat rocks because it's easier to do the turn-arounds in Tai Chi on level rock instead of a bumpy meadow. A favorite outcrop of rock, laid down ages ago by geological processes, is near the highway under Grand Turk. Because the rock holds the heat, the snow melts along the edge exposed to the sun, providing the perfect spot for this early spring photo.

The clear air, the glistening warm rock and the towering mass of Grand Turk just above – all combine to increase the chi energy. Jodi almost takes off to fly just as the stork.

Form 10, Stork Spreads Its Wings. This form's name comes from the fact that storks "move sedately as they walk...their long, broad wings have slow deliberate, beats", as *The Birds of North America* text explains. The form lifts the chest and the arms, revolving round the spine, increasing chi flow. In this form, the right hand guides the chi from the *tan tien* up to the head and then brings the chi back down to the *tan tien* in a continuous flow.

Mountains loom upon the path we take;
Yonder peak rises sharp and clear;
Behold. It stands with its head uplifted...

Tahirussawichi – from the Hako, sacred land ritual of the
Pawnee tribe recorded by Fletcher in 1898.

In Brush Knee and Twist Step, Jodi's hands alternately interact with heaven and earth in each movement, as her hands change from yin to yang, while she moves below the "Higher Power", Engineer Peak, above. Her arms alternately mirror the ridges of the mountain as she moves through the radiant early morning light. "Chinese thought refused to separate Man from Nature...the gods are seen as immanent natural forces, not as transcendent superhuman beings." (Joseph Needham). A similar concept is found in many primitive cultures as documented by Alice Fletcher, an early American ethnologist, who spent 25 years with various tribes during the late 1880s. For the Omaha tribe, Wakonda was the "Great Power" and among the Pawnee, Tirawa Atius was the "Mighty Power". There were other powers: the sun, the stars, and the moon, but "these were lesser powers." The Sioux, Vine Deloria (1991) defines the "Higher Powers" connected with particular locations. He explains that the Higher Powers are in communication with human beings through continuous ceremonies held at particular locations on the land which "provide the people with the necessary information to enable them to maintain a balance in their relationships with the earth and other forms of life." Similarly, in Japan certain natural beings such as trees, rocks, and mountains, with special Power are called *Kami*.

This peak (altitude 12,968 ft.) was named "Engineer" by Lt. Ernest Ruffner of the Army Corps of Engineers expedition in 1873 to locate the l07th meridian to set the boundary for the Ute Indian reservation. As the highway climbs up out of Silverton valley the peak suddenly appears, standing alone below the open sky. The mountain has been carved by grinding glaciers into the horn shape – similar to the famous Matterhorn in Switzerland. Pennsylvania marine sediments form the lower slopes of Engineer Mt. Pennsylvanian and Permian redbeds – sandstone and shale, washed from the ancient Uncompahgre – form the higher slopes. The cliff bands on the right side of the mountain are made up of igneous, Tertiary rock. Engineer is capped by a lacolith of a harder quartz type rock. The horn type of mountain is the ultimate expression of the snow flakes such as those which fall on Silverton in the winter. When more snow accumulates than can melt in a summer, we have the beginnings of glaciers and when glaciers grow big enough they begin moving and carving out the mountains. Glaciers, in valleys on separate sides of the mountain, carving away at the mountain, eventually create these elegant horn shapes.

Forms 13 to 15, Brush Knee and Twist Step, circulates chi energy throughout the body.

> **A thing is right when it tends to preserve the integrity,
> stability and beauty of the biotic community.
> It is wrong when it tends otherwise.**
> *Aldo Leopold*

At the conclusion of our early spring photo, Jodi reaches out in gratitude to embrace the two buttresses lying at the base of Grand Turk. She holds them in relationship just as she holds the varied types of people in our small town together in her Avalanche Cafe.

Jodi got her B.A. degree from the University of Wisconsin in "Biological Aspects of Conservation", a course designed by Aldo Leopold. She moved out to Colorado because of her love for mountains.

Al Chung-liang Huang tells us that long ago when he studied Tai Chi in China among the mountains, his master told him: "Flow down. Hold the mountain and carry it home. Return. You have known the outer mountain, experienced it... . Now, take it home, return, return to your center, your lower base, your tan tien...return to your own Inner Mountain."

The chi energy Jodi gets from this mountain not only helps her hold the people together within our town but also helps them to balance their energy with the powerful San Juan mountains surrounding us.

These buttresses were carved by the glacier, just as was Grand Turk above them. The space between contained highly metamorphosed rock. Glaciers don't carve such loose rock, they pluck it out, leaving a gap.

In this March photo the early spring sun on the rock has melted much of the snow. The two buttresses mirror the equal yin and yang, which occurs at the Spring equinox. At that time yin and yang are equal; thereafter the yang continues to grow until Summer solstice. The equinoxes are the balance points of the wheel of the year.

Form 21, Embrace Tiger, Return to Mountain is the conclusion of Section I of Tai Chi. Tiger stands for chi energy.

"Overflowing abundance of water gushes from between red cliffs and pours out. 'In the gift of the outpouring, earth and sky, divinities and mortals dwell together...'"

Martin Heidegger

In the San Juan Mountains, full spring arrives late. With the month of June, life bursts forth in overflowing abundance. Jodi opens her arms, palms up to the sky, gathering all the chi energy from sky and earth and falling water. In the "Return to Mountain" form here in our San Juan Mountains, Jodi helps us understand how the pilgrimage called "opening of the spring peak" ceremony brings together the yin (earth) and yang (sky), the powers of the four directions and the "root traces", coming out of the "primordial potentiality" of the spring season. The "opening of the peak ceremony" comes from the Shugendo tradition in Japan, which absorbed "the ancient Japanese tradition and blended it with Taoist and Buddhist conceptions." Shugendo involves pilgrimages into the mountains to take part in the mountain powers. Those who follow this "way" are called *yamabushi*, meaning "those who sleep in the mountains."

In Embrace Tiger, Return to Mountain, Jodi's feet are deeply rooted like a tree while her body is supple as a willow. The muscles are relaxed, the support coming from the tendons which distribute the weight of the body evenly through the feet to the rock below. The crucial spot for balance is the "Gushing Spring" acupuncture point between the two pads directly behind the toes. The meridians for the major organs of the body cross at this point, allowing chi energy from the earth below to penetrate. This balance point is called the "sweet spot" by skiers.

Form 21 – Embrace Tiger, Return to Mountain. Tiger refers to energy and in this form all the energy generated during Tai Chi is gathered (embrace tiger) and brought to the tan tien (return to mountain).

This series of photos along South Mineral Creek mark the culmination of Section One of Tai Chi. To celebrate this culmination, Jodi does the forms of Section One in three different places along the creek, ending each section with Form 21. Form 21 has three aspects: 1) gathering chi from above, 2) gathering chi from all around her as she does the form and 3) returning all the chi to the tan tien, the mountain within. This photo shows the first aspect, gathering chi from the sky.

The fecund Spring pours out its gifts.
All nature radiates a kind of glory.
Anonymous from the Han Dynasty

Gathering in all the chi energy while continuing Embrace Tiger, Return to Mountain, Jodi lets her arms move out, embracing all the chi energy around her as her eyes rest on the tops of the trees splashed by early morning sunlight.

The foam, rising from the waterfall below, shines in the rising sun. Because of the mist created by this series of waterfalls, the micro-climate is more like the Pacific Northwest than dry Southwest Colorado. Moss hangs in the trees and wood nymph plants blossom beneath them. Dotted saxifrage hangs along the cliff edges. Its roots creep into the crevices and slowly decompose the rock by chemical action; the dead plant parts gradually decay and form organic food materials for new growth. This tiny flower, about as big as a small finger nail, actually breaks the rock. Saxifrage derives from the Latin *sax* meaning rock and *frag* as in fragment (break).

In the reciprocal appropriation of this place, the saxifrage roots break the rock to make soil, South Mineral Creek provides the water for plants, animals and humans, and Jodi returns reverence to this place. The deep gorges of this area hold the winter snow and release it slowly – some snowbanks last well into August.

The Japanese would call a place with such Power, "*Kami*". The word *kami*, originally meant "over, above." Eventually, this was extended to objects above their surroundings such as mountains. Generally it came to mean that which was "superior but not immortal, omniscient or possessed with infinite power."

"Not only humans but birds, beasts, plants and trees, seas and mountains and all other things whatsoever which deserve to be revered for the extraordinary and preeminent powers which they possess, are called kami." This does not mean that a spirit is in the tree or waterfall etc.; but that the mountain or sea or tree itself is kami. Such a concept results in the feeling of "a sense of deep reverence for the forces of nature, which are always present in a diffuse state, but sometimes manifest themselves at a higher potential".

Form 21 – Embrace Tiger, Return to Mountain. Jodi's arms have moved down to begin gathering all the chi around her.

" Mountains and rivers compel me to speak for them;
They are transformed through me and
I am transformed through them. "

Shih-T'ao (Ming Dynasty)

Jodi has just gathered all the chi energy and raised it to heart level. Now she lowers her arms and straightens her legs so the chi energy moves into the tan tien, as she gazes in awe at the combination of sacred landscape forms in this place.

The nourishing mother goddess form is seen through the cleft in the tree-filled little gorge. The Mother Mountain reaches out her arms (the lower ridges) to embrace the world below. In ancient Crete, in Greece and in Japan such a mountain shows the caring, nurturing aspect. In Greece she was called Artemis, the one who sheltered birds, snakes, and all wild things beneath her arms. She is truly nourishing because such a form was created by glaciers, thus providing soil.

The waterfall just below Jodi is a sacred landscape form called "the vagina of the earth" – the gushing abundance of the water given to us by earth and sky together.

Heidegger says that the earth, the sky, the gods and the mortals together make the culture of a particular place. The European language calls them gods. But, as the Heidegger scholar Vycinas explains: Actually gods, "are disclosed as powers which are embedded in the eternal play of Nature." In his book on Chaung Tzu, Kuang Ming-Wu says "Let us play our lives and our world together." Play implies free movement of Nature's forces and humans within nature and not narrow rational control by the human mind alone.

Form 21 – Embrace Tiger, Return to Mountain – concluding part of this form.

> *"...every needle thrilling and singing and shedding off keen lances of light like a diamond..."*
> *John Muir*

Jodi has moved a little higher above the waterfall, doing another Embrace Tiger conclusion for Section l. Her arms are just beginning to move down to gather chi energy from all around her.

The glowing green tips of the tree give off negative ions, adding to those given off by the falling water. Early morning light shows through her fingers, playing on the water below her.

Again we have nature's "playing powers". This Power flows through animals, plants, waterfalls, mountains and humans in endless abundance. For example, when I am skiing with no effort, I feel that it's not me skiing. I'm not doing it; instead, *It* skis me. Whenever something is going very well with no effort, most of us have the feeling that its not us doing it, but that "the powers" are skiing us or playing us. That's "the sacred."

Tai Chi places one into this larger "more-than-human" feeling and out of the limited left hemisphere rational thinking. And, as Bateson says: "one of the very curious things about the sacred is that it usually does not make sense to the left-hemisphere type of thinking..."

Form 21 – Embrace Tiger, Return to Mountain. Jodi's arms are moving down from gathering chi from above toward gathering chi all around.

"*The life of these Indians is nothing but a continuous religious experience...The spirit of wonder, the recognition of life as power, as a mysterious. ubiquitous, concentrated form of nonmaterial energy, of something loose about the world and contained in a more or less condensed degree by every object – this is the credo of the Pit River Indians.*"

Jaime de Angulo

Jodi gathers the chi energy from all around her as she watches the wave above the falls curl over, back and crest. With each rippling response of the waters to the sunlight, spring is growing ever stronger.

Form 21 – Embrace Tiger, Return to Mountain.

Embrace Tiger, Return to Mountai

The wild is neither a controlled mechanism nor random chaos. It is a mysterious living, creative process in which we participate with myriad beings. We should express our gratitude to it for being given the gift of life.
Alan Drengson

Jodi begins the third Embrace Tiger at still another place along the creek, her arms reaching toward the heavens to begin accumulating chi energy from above. The wilderness within her, the tan tien, meets the wilderness without, experiencing "the binding and interconnecting thread of the presence of the sacred. In terms of interconnections, a dominant theme in all Native American cultures is that of relationships." Elaine Jahner explains further that this occurs not only among humans but extends "out to embrace and relate to the environment. Associated with relationship is the theme of reciprocity. Put very simply, reciprocity here refers to that process wherein if you receive or take away you must also give back."

Form 21 – The beginning move of the last of the three Embrace Tiger, Return to Mountain conclusions for Section I.

Embrace Tiger, Return to Mountain

The Spirit of Restoration that we need to embody...what we are restoring is relationships – with each other and with real living places, each with its own set of unique ecologies, hydrologies, histories, and cranky psychologies.

Freeman House

Jodi continues the form from the previous photo, spreading her arms widely to gather in all the surrounding chi energy. She celebrates with reverence the many lives in this place – from the tiny dotted saxifrage to trees above them and even to the very ancient Cutler Sandstone. Her feet are rooted to this ancient rock as her arms continue the slow movement down.

The red rock of the Cutler Formation was formed from small grains of sands deposited by streams during the Permian era and then compressed over eons. Now in our time, the fine grained Cutler rock creates elegant curved forms as the water cuts through it. This Cutler Formation extends all the way to Canyonlands in Utah.

Form 21 – Embrace Tiger, Return to Mountain, continued.

In breathing one must proceed (as follows). One holds (the breath) and it is collected together. If it is collected it expands. When it expands it goes down. When it goes down it becomes quiet. When it becomes quiet it will solidify. When it becomes solidified it will begin to sprout. After it has sprouted it will grow. As it grows it will be pulled back again (to the upper regions). When it has been pulled back it will reach the crown of the head. Above it will press against the crown of the head. Below, it will press downward. Whoever follows this will live; whoever acts contrary to it will die.

Inscription on twelve pieces of jade, which may have formed part of the knob of a staff (dating back to the middle of the 6th century BC)

Jodi concludes the final move in the form, Embrace Tiger, Return to Mountain. Having embraced all the chi energy and returned it to her heart level she now straightens her arms and and pushes down, thus returning the chi to her tan tien. The soles of her feet interact with the rock, gathering more chi energy.

Breathing exercises for the tan tien go back to very ancient times in China. The tan tien is located about 4 fingers (2 inches) below the navel. This Tai Chi type of breathing increases the movement of chi energy from the upper part of the body down to the abdomen where the major organs lie. Also the chi energy continues down to the soles of the feet where the "gushing spring" acupuncture point lies and thus the internal organs are replenished directly from the flow of chi energy. The breath moving down expands the abdomen outward - no forcing - just filling it with breath like blowing up a balloon.

This form of breathing is also called embryo breathing - the way we breathed when inside our mother – original nourishment. In the Tai Chi form of breathing the older brains in the head and the old brain in the tan tien reach a state of quietude. The rational hemisphere is totally bypassed and life flows through us, unimpeded.

Form 21 – Embrace Tiger, Return to Mountain. Conclusion of Section I.

夏

Summer

On the summer solstice, the sun reaches its northernmost setting point on the horizon. The following day it begins its journey back along the horizon to its winter setting point. Summer solstice is the longest day of the year.

In China, which has the longest continuous record of seasonal rituals, *The Book of Records* tells of instructions which "the Perfect Emperor Yao (2254 BC) gave to his astronomers to ascertain the solstices and equinoxes...and fix the four seasons..."

Traditionally, in Celtic countries bonfires were lit on Summer solstice. At this time the people felt that the energy of the sun needed to be renewed as it began its long journey back to its "winter house." To be precise, winter really begins on summer solstice day. This is when the yin energy, although totally hidden in the brightness and warmth of summer, begins to grow, increasing in strength until Winter solstice. Yang energy begins to decrease. This change does not seem quite as perilous as the change-over from yin to yang at the winter solstice, because at summer solstice it is warm and sunny, while in the winter people feel anxious at the growing cold and dark even though the sun (yang) is beginning to grow stronger.

The Celtic bonfires were lit "to protect from...evil influences, and to ensure the well-being of the sun in its course in the heavens.." Many traditional cultures had their World Renewal Rites at this time to renew the energy of the sun, the vegetation and the people. Various cultures have a special festival when the sound of thunder is first heard. Thunder and lightning and the coming of fertilizing rain signal a periodic return to the "chaos time" and the resulting new creation and rebirth. This was true in ancient China and much of the Taoist writings about Lord Hun-Tun, "chaos" have to do with thunder. "The magic and ritual power of drums was associated with the power to reproduce the thunder of the creation time." Chanting and ritual dancing (a precursor of Tai Chi) also took place at this time.

Here in the San Juan mountains in late June at summer solstice time the mountain wildflowers are bursting forth. Some have not bloomed yet because the snow just melted in those areas, while nearby, often the snow has not yet melted at all and can still be several feet deep. Yet the sun is warm and the air is delightful. We are surrounded by rapidly growing vegetation and early blooming flowers.

> *Tai Chi on the mountain's flank*
> *high above the dark valley, roots thrust*
> *deep in rock, I grasp clouds*
> *ancient motifs of Taoist monks…*
> Mike Adams

Summer solstice! We take advantage of the few days of perfect weather between springtime and the wild mountain thunderstorms of July. We go up to Stony Pass, the High Divide (12,588 ft.) we can see from down here in Silverton. When we get to the top of the pass we find among the remaining snowbanks an immense diversity of plants just beginning to push up under the incredibly clear, blue sky.

Jodi moves along the narrow ridge just above the Pass, on the lower slopes of Green Mountain (13,049 ft.). On one side of her the ridge drops off steeply toward the Rio Grande River, beginning its 1865 mile journey to the Gulf of Mexico and the Atlantic Ocean. On the other side of her, sheer rock cliffs lead down to our home valley of the Animas River, which eventually drains into the Colorado River and on into the Pacific Ocean. There's 1300 miles between the mouths of these rivers, which begin exactly here, where Jodi moves between the two oceans far away and far below our mountains.

Our local history is intimately linked with Stony Pass. Beginning about 1871, most of the early prospectors came through Stony Pass on their way to the newly found mining area of what was then known as Baker's Park (now Silverton). During the succeeding decades enormous quantities of heavy mining equipment were loaded on burros and freighted through this pass from the Rio Grande River in the San Luis Valley. Once over the pass they had to wend their way among the precipitous cliffs above the Animas drainage. These long strings of burros carried in everything needed in Baker's Park until the railroad, coming up the Animas River valley from Durango, reached Silverton in 1882.

Form 33 – Brush Knee and Twist Step. During the Season of Summer Jodi does forms from Section II and III of Tai Chi.

*When the ancient Chinese speak of the relationship between
heaven and earth creating their world, they use the word,
Tien, for heaven: 'They are aware of all that is enclosed within
the hallowed conception of Tien, which is not the heaven we
know, but the mysterious government of the blue sky at noon.
It is a world... of... pure intensity.'*
Robert Payne

Jodi continues doing Brush Knee and Twist Step along the High Divide ridge
of Green Mountain under the radiant expanse of blue sky on a perfect day at
high altitude.

Blue Sky, *Skan*, is one of the Four Great Powers which make up the Great
Mystery of the Sioux. The other Powers are the Rock (*Inyan*), the Earth and the
Sun. For the Skidi Pawnee, the blue sky is *Tirawahat*. Her Pawnee informant
told Fletcher that "when you look up you shall call the sky *Ti-ra-wa-hat*." The
universe and the sky were thought of as being synonymous. *Tirawahat* was ever
present in all things. "When he wept it rained; the white of his eyes was the place
where the sky touches the earth from which clouds rise."

Our Green Mountain has a similar geographical/cultural location as the
famous Mt. Kailas in the Himalayas which is considered the most sacred
mountain of the world, revered by Hindus, Buddhists and Jains. Two mighty
rivers, the Indus and the Brahmaputra, have their source here. Traversing the
whole of the Indian subcontinent, the Indus flows into the Arabian Sea to the
west and the Brahmaputra flows into the Bay of Bengal to the east of India.
Both of these are actually part of the same Indian Ocean. The rivers flowing
from our Green Mountain go into two *separate* oceans – the Atlantic and the
Pacific Oceans.

Form 46 – Brush Knee and Twist Step.

Hither winds, come to us
Come oh winds come
Now the winds come to us
Lo the winds round us sweep
Safe now are we
By the winds safe.

Pawnee chant to Hotoru, the Wind Power

Jodi continues Brush Knee and Twist Step, surrounded by the Powers, which are building up chi energy and negative ions within her, under the great pure sky.

Form 46 – Brush Knee and Twist Step (left). In this form the hips control the rotating of the entire upper torso around the spine. The spine transfers power from the hips throughout the body. Her body remains at the same level throughout the entire move; only her legs bend and straighten with each step forward. As her toes alternately point straight ahead and then turn out on the heel, her tendons stretch and contract, helping to move chi energy throughout the body.

Brush knee and
Twist Step

"To soar and roam is an enjoyment of life that is not, mind you, a violent excitement but a daily routine, the constant Tao of things. To soar is to live in the perspective of the sky. To roam is to rise and fly with things. Not to soar and roam is to suffer in life. To soar and roam (hsiao yao) is to leisurely frolic (yu) as a mole who knows his river and his place in it. Such a place is forever shifting, sometimes into sunny comfort, sometimes into dark hazards."

Kuang-Ming Wu's commentary on Chuang Tzu's Chapter One – "Soaring and Roaming".

Jodi continues Brush Knee and Twist Step. A step on either side of the narrow ridge would put her in our home valley, draining to the Pacific Ocean, or in the Rio Grande drainage, emptying into the Atlantic Ocean.

Many things from the largest – the galaxies – to the smallest, the DNA molecule in the gene cell (the key to the mystery of reproduction and the processes of life) – have the form of a spiral helix. In Brush Knee and Twist Step Jodi moves in a helical way. Her right foot is placed on the tundra, then she rotates on her heel, turning the foot out toward the Animas River and she puts her weight on it. Then the left foot is put forward and she turns her foot out toward the Rio Grande River. Every movement made to the right is followed with one to the left. The yin and yang are continually interacting. She turns one palm up to the sky, preparatory to a large circular motion which leads to the palm parallel with the tundra and then turning up into a push, using tendon action. This is followed by the same move with the other palm, again right and left hands in a yin and yang movement.

Jodi moves through Alpine Buttercups, which are found only around timberline and above. Exposed to severe climatic conditions, a short season and temperatures sometimes below freezing at night, they must grow and mature quickly. Often they bloom as soon as the snow melts, sometimes even pushing up through the snow. "Heat given off during respiration of a growing plant is sufficient to melt a hole one inch or so in diameter."

Form 46 – Brush Knee and Twist Step (right).

I, however, as one who blesses and affirms if only you are around me, you pure, luminous sky! You abyss of light – then into all abysses do I carry my concentrating affirmation!
Nietzsche

Jodi continues along the narrow High Divide ridge amidst the glowing light of the later afternoon sun.

A subsidiary ridge looms behind her with a narrow ribbon of snow along it. This is a remnant of the cornice, still lingering at summer solstice. Such cornices are built up by fierce winds moving up the slope and then at the top, the lee, the wind-blown snow drops out and is deposited in a deep cornice, sometimes 50 or more feet deep. Even the hot summer sun cannot melt all of it quickly. This slowly melting cornice serves as a reservoir of snow continually replenishing the Rio Grande River far below and helping to water the crops way down stream in New Mexico and even clear to Texas.

Form 46 – Brush Knee and Twist Step (left).

Brush knee and
Twist Step

"The experience of mountains cannot be bought, it can only be lived, a lasting tie of blood and bone, a fever that once contracted cannot be cured, a sensation along the spine that endures long after the transitory adrenaline high of packaged thrills and advertised adventures."

Harry Middleton

The sun set behind an intervening ridge just as we finished the previous photo, so we went up again the next day to finish the sequence. Here in the open meadow below the ridge line, Jodi moves through alpine flowers doing Brush Knee and Twist Step facing our home valley of the Animas River.

Behind her in the distance one can look down into the upper reaches of the Rio Grande and on to the further range of mountains which enclose the other side of that drainage.

The famous philosopher Santayana spoke of the Power which mountains exert on us, when he gave a speech at the University of California in 1911. He said: "In their non-human beauty and peace they stir the sub-human depths and superhuman possibilities of your own spirit." He went on to say that they don't teach philosophy or logic but rather they demonstrate "the vanity and superficiality of all logic, the needlessness of argument, the finitude of mortals, the strength of time, the fertility of matter, the variety, the unspeakable variety of possible life." If philosophers had lived among the mountains their systems would have been different from those systems "which the European Genteel Tradition has handed down since Socrates." The Genteel Tradition is "inspired by the conceited notion that man, or human reason...is the center and pivot of the universe. That is what the mountains and the woods should make you at last ashamed to assert." Mountains "suspend your forced sense of your importance not merely as individuals, but even as men. They allow you, in one happy moment, at once to play and worship...and to salute the wild, indifferent, non-censorious infinity of nature."

Form 46 – Brush Knee and Twist Step

Brush knee and
Twist Step

"Verily, one alone of all these was the greatest.
Inspiring to all...
The great rock...
In the midst of the winds you sit
Aged one...
He! This is the desire of your little ones
That of your strength they shall partake
Therefore your little ones desire
to walk closely by your side
Venerable one!"
Omaha Tribal Chant

Jodi does the concluding form, Embrace Tiger, Return to Mountain for this sequence at Stony Pass, embracing all the chi energy and the negative ions and the Power of the great rock. For this form she has moved further up the ridge separating the Animas and the Rio Grande and moves beneath the monolithic rock which dominates the ridge.

Arne Naess, founder of Deep Ecology and a Himalayan mountaineer, writes about "a way of understanding ourselves as part of nature in a wide sense of the term. This way is such that the smaller we come to feel ourselves compared to the mountain, the nearer we come to participating in its greatness. I do not know why this is so."

Inyan, the Rock, is one of the four aspects of The Great Mystery of the Sioux, mentioned earlier. The other three are *Skan* (blue sky), earth and the sun. Lame Deer says:"*Inyan* – the rocks – are holy. Every man needs a stone to help him...Deep inside you there must be an awareness of the rock power, otherwise you would not pick them up and fondle them as you do."

Yuichiro Miura, who skied down Everest and whose ancestors were Shinto priests, gives us another aspect of Rock Power and Mountain Power: "I was alone on the South Col saddle, a tiny speck amidst the white expanse...The Mountain taught me the real identity of a man named Yuichiro Miura...The sole meaning of one's existence – whether on the highest peak or in the lowliest of pursuits – is not to understand life, or mold it, or change it, or even really love it...but rather to drink deep of its underlying essence."

Form 60 – Embrace Tiger, Return to Mountain

“ *Alongside the peaks they tread emptiness. *”*
Alan Grapard, “Flying Mountains and Walkers of Emptiness.”

Jodi moves within "the fullness of the void" of the early morning fog. She rotates about her spine. Her lower body faces front while her upper body rotates at right angles to promote chi flow. Her left hand guides the chi from the upper left down to the right side of her body, followed by the right hand moving up from the lower left and moving in a circular mode to the upper right, then down again to the tan tien. With each movement of her arms she steps sideways in this "cloud dance."

The fog which has formed above the Animas River is beginning to rise and disperse due to the warming effects of the early morning sun. As the fog moves upwards it gradually hides the trees on the lower ridges of Grand Turk. The rising sun has not yet reached Jodi on the lower slopes of Kendall Mountain.

There is a stone engraving in an early Tang tomb (618–906), where three pairs of female dancers do exactly this same cloud hands movement; thus this form has come down to us unchanged for over a thousand years.

Moving effortlessly, Jodi rotates freely about her spine while doing Cloud Hands, allowing chi energy to move through her spinal artery. Chuang Tzu has a story about this movement. He says that the hinge of a door can begin to function only when it is fitted into the middle of the socket. The hinge of The Way (The Tao) can "respond infinitely and freely to endlessly changing situations of the phenomenal world" only when it is free to move without the restrictions of rational thinking. Lao Tzu explained: "Man stands in a woeful predicament because he is so made that he directs the activity of his mind toward distinguishing and discriminating things from one another." In Cloud Hands this narrow human-centered, rational discrimination is totally bypassed as the body moves slowly through the changing void of the clouds. Things appear and disappear and mountains seem to fly as Jodi "treads emptiness".

Form 40 – Wave Hands Like Clouds (right)

Wave Hands Like Clouds

*The hills waver in and out of the fog,
liquidating / materializing:
a choreography of rock.*
Robert MacLean

Continuing Cloud Hands, Jodi's arms move in the opposite direction, continuing to rotate about her spine as the rocks of Anvil Mountain appear and disappear, seeming to fly as the dispersing fog moves among them.

In Japan the beauty and mystery of dispersing fog among the mountains provided the inspiration for the early Buddhist legends of Chinese sacred mountains flying to Japan. The Japanese Buddhists no longer had to go to China to visit these sacred mountains; instead the mountains flew to them. For example in the year 933 a Japanese master wrote down a statement which had been handed down from master to master: "A long time ago there was in China a mountain called Kimpusen, residence of the Bodhisattva Zao. However, this mountain came flying to Japan…it approached as if floating over the ocean."

The cold water of our mountain stream, the Animas River, throws enough moisture into the air to lower the air temperature to where dew forms and becomes fog. The heat of the rising sun generates convection, which mixes the warmer air above with the colder air lying along the Animas River and the fog begins to disperse. "Clouds in the stratus family that lie on the ground are called fog" is the scientific definition of fog. When one is within the fog it has no form but as it moves and disperses various things such as trees, rocks, mountains etc. appear and disappear. This phenomenon led the early Taoists to use the term "the fullness of the void" out of which all things come.

Form 40 – Wave Hands Like Clouds (left).

Wave Hands Like Clouds

" *To drift like clouds and flow like water.* "
Ancient Chinese poem

Jodi concludes the Cloud Hands sequence. It is one of the most powerful forms of Tai Chi because it shows how the very slow but linked consecutive movements seem to hold time in abeyance. The photos of this sequence draw the viewer into the slow movement itself so that one participates in the reciprocal appropriation of Jodi "soaring and roaming" within all the life around her.

Chuang Tzu often writes of "soaring and roaming." This is the title of his first chapter. Kuang-Ming Wu explains that roaming (*yu*) is not to be confused with repetition. Repetition results from remembering and comparing past events and comes to mean we are trapped in the cyclical recurrences of the same old thing. Roaming, *yu*, "does not remember, compare, and judge, but merely lives the now to the full, before going to the next 'now'."

Wu asks the rhetorical question. "But what about suffering?" He points out that although Chuang Tzu deals with suffering in almost every chapter, he doesn't consider it the major issue of life. Wu explains further that "suffering was not for him the central concern, as it was for Buddha; nor was suffering an important issue for Chuang Tzu, as it was for Jesus. Buddha came to solve *the* problem of suffering, of which Jesus came to make a redemptive use. For Chuang Tzu suffering is a mishandling of life; the *problem* of suffering is itself a mistake. "Suffering is not to be solved but to be let be, to dissolve of itself." It's like the early morning fog when the sun warms the air.

Summing up, Wu states: "To live rightly is neither living redemptively (Jesus) nor living enlightenedly (Buddha), but living appropriately, that is, fittingly to the changing climate of things, now soaring, now roaming – and that is Chuang Tzu's central concern." Instead of the usual idea of heroes enduring suffering in order to live happily ever after, Chuang Tzu's writings "are themselves moving images of happiness *amidst* suffering, happiness that is as nonchalant as animals and trees." He recommends soaring and roaming "*with* the seasonal winds of this world."

Form 40 – Wave Hands Like Clouds (right).

> *Heaven and earth and the natural seasons 'move' according to a prescribed order and according to this 'movement' new phenomena or 'root-traces' are born...*
> *Ansho Togawa*

Jodi has climbed up among the roots. With one foot on the earth and one foot on the giant roots, she drops into Snake Creeps Down. This form opens up the entire lower part of the body to increase the chi energy flow between her and the tree and the earth itself.

In the Snake Creeps Down form of Tai Chi we have links clear back to the ancient myths of the entire Southern Austronesian cultural sources and the serpent goddess, Nu-kua. She was the goddess of the legendary Hsia Kingdom of China (about 2000 B.C.) In much later times, the Taoist Lao Tzu, in the *Tao Te Ching* evoked the "profound female" who was the "valley spirit who never dies," providing another link with the ancient Nu-kua. Nu-Kua, the serpent goddess is "linked with the legendary Yellow Emperor as the great 'transformer', and in another passage she is presented as the repairer of heaven and earth with multicolored stones after a great catastrophe." She is associated with the idea of "transformation of the continuous creation and regeneration of the world." It's most appropriate that Jodi does this form within tree roots, which continually push their way among the stones, breaking them and eventually forming soil, out of which more trees can grow in a "continous creation" of life. For these ancient peoples, the fact that snakes shed their old skin and continuously grow a new skin led to the concept of the snake as a symbol of eternal life.

This concept of the tree roots breaking the rock, the rock crumbling away into soil and the tree dying and all this, together, creating new soil which will bring new life has deep implications for us. As Freeman House says: "Once we have begun this process of remembering we will find that the instructions for the reclamation of our human destinies lie in our direct perception of the self-regenerating processes of the landscape that surrounds us." Tai Chi sharpens these perceptions in all ways –through the senses, through the skin and through the body with chi energy.

Form 78 – Snake Creeps Down.

> *The Blue Dragon from the Court of Fire descends to meet the White Tiger from the Abyss of Water. Thus the polarities of Yin and Yang are united and the Golden Flower blooms.*
>
> Ancient Chinese saying

The dragon and the serpent have similar meanings in Chinese symbolism. In Tai Chi the Court of Fire is the heart area, the Abyss of Water is where the *tan tien*, the other brain, lies. When these two energies combine then the "Golden Flower blooms."

In this closer view of Jodi within one of the coils of the tree root, the tree rises directly above her. In Tai Chi the body is rooted deeply into the earth below like tree roots extending down into the earth; while the upper body moves loosely and freely just as a willow blowing in the wind.

The tan tien, sometimes called the "sacred middle", is the area where the flow of energy takes place between us and the cosmos. The functions of sex, prenatal life, birth, assimilation of food as well as deep emotions all take place in this area. The "sacred middle" refers to the sacrum, the bony plate which gets its name from the same Latin root as the word, sacred. In ancient times the Romans practiced divining the future by throwing the sacrum from a sheep into the fire and later taking it out to "read" the cracks which had developed.

All the muscles involved in walking, standing and sitting converge in the "sacred middle". Of these muscles, the psoas muscles are the most important for determining the human, upright position; while the pubo-coccygeus muscles, which attach the legs to the inner side of the spine and run up to fasten the pelvic rim to the front of the ribs and the breastbone, literally hold us together. Both these large strong sets of muscles crisscross in the pelvic area, circling around the sexual organs. The form Snake Creeps Down opens up this entire area to the flow of chi energy.

Jodi's right foot is resting directly on the root so that her "Gushing Spring" acupuncture point, which is "the center of the foot where the root lies", is directly connected with the tree root. As mentioned before, the Gushing Spring is the common point where many acupuncture meridians cross on the sole of the foot.

Form 78 – Snake Creeps Down.

> *Lao Tzu says: 'The Return to the Root is to be called Stillness…'*
> *The vital energy hidden in the darkness of the root is actually*
> *motionless, but the root is by no means dead. It is, rather, a*
> *stillness pregnant with infinite vitality. Externally no movement*
> *is perceptible, yet internally the incessant movement of eternal*
> *life is carried on in preparation for the coming season.*
> Toshihiko Izutsu

Jodi sinks down into "stillness" between the roots as she begins Snake Creeps Down. Her breath sinks right down into her fully open *tan tien* filling it with chi energy.

"[T]o come home to one's nature is for each self to return to its root, returning to the Primitive through non-doing, to its own unwrought Simplicity…to act naturally of oneself, from the very nature of oneself. It is the natural way to go back to Life." Kuang Ming-Wu continues, "If I am under the authority of the Root-power of life…I owe it to myself to return to my root, to my pristine simplicity, and to live accordingly… ." In Chuang Tzu's view this leads "to the universal unification of natural selfishness with the ideal society. Come home to your inborn root-nature and things and people will grow and thrive of themselves. Stop being natural, and then even one's own six bodily apertures shall fight one against another, not to speak of one's quarrels with neighbors…As I go back to my root that is the Other, I go back to primordial sociality that is togetherness of one another."

In this close-up photo we can see some of the "natural sociality" inherent in this small area. Mychorizae root fungus helps the roots absorb nutrients for the tree. Roots draw up negative ions from the earth and send them through the tree to come out the foliate tips thus making humans feel good. Roots bring up water for the tree and provide us with oxygen. In return we provide the tree with carbon dioxide. Roots stabilize the tree in the powerful mountain winds. The tree's needles eventually fall, providing more nutrients.

Scattered on the ground, we see coarse woody debris, providing long-term sources of nutrients for the tree as well as providing food, shelter, protection, cover, and substrate or climate amelioration for many species.

Form 78 – Snake Creeps Down.

*" **Fragrant breeze, Summer!** "*

Completing the long series of backward moves for the Repulse Monkey form, Jodi turns to the right, stepping out on her right foot. Her right arm moves up, as her left arms moves down much as a bird's wings slant as it turns in the air; thus the name, Slanting Flying. Her palm reaches up toward the sky, making a continuous flow of chi energy from her palm down to the toes of her back foot.

In Standing Flying, there's a moment just at the crest where her arm and palm have created a timeless non-doing. Then gravity takes over and pulls her arm down and her body settles downward into the rock. When there is no focusing of the will on what we would attain, the human senses are fully disposed to perceive the world and to receive it as Jodi shows when she cradles her surrounding world in the palm of her hand. The joy of receiving this lush meadow with hundreds of roots in the earth and hundreds of blades of green extending up into the air, in the overflowing abundance of summer, leads to a continuous flow of chi energy. The predominant plant in this meadow is the Indian paintbrush which is a semiparasite, making only a portion of its food directly. The rest comes from its strategy of sending roots into the soil until they touch the roots of other plants, usually perennials, and then they penetrate into the host plant to steal some of its food. This is a useful strategy for high altitude annuals where the growing season is so short. Alpine meadows need many such cooperative arrangements. The color in the paintbrush plant doesn't come from the blossom, but the bracts. The actual blossoms are narrow, green tubular spikes at the top of the unbranched stem. These are seldom noticed because they are hidden by the flamboyant bracts, but occasionally one can see a bee sucking nectar from the end of this slender tube.

The microbiologist Lynn Margulis tells us that "every organism is part of a larger ecosystem, a system on which it depends for respiratory gas, water, food, and a sink for waste products. Are bacteria 'public-spirited' in ridding themselves of their waste, which happens to be the oxygen necessary for other organisms in the system... . With the exception of bacteria, individuals with single genetic systems don't exist. All other living organisms, such as animals, plants, and fungi are complex communities of multiple, tightly organized beings... . It's not the individual but the community of life that evolves by cooperation, interaction, mutual dependence. Life did not take over the globe by combat but by networking."

Form 21 – Standing Flying.

> **And the multi-colored flowers
> Inch out of the shadow.**

Jodi has just turned around doing the form, Single Whip. Suddenly, she is pulled into the grandeur of deep space up towards the High Divide. Behind her the lower peaks move in and out of the cloud shadows playing over the ridges and highlighting the banks of deep snow still remaining from winter. These pockets of snow are formed by wind blowing up and over subsidiary ridges and piling up the wind-drifted snow on the lee side.

Jodi is surrounded by an unusual mass of flowers because this area is to the lee of the nearby ridge and benefits from the increased snow accumulation dropping out as it comes over to the lee side. Thus this area is not blasted by icy winds but instead is blessed with consistent water as the deep snow pockets gradually melt out.

High alpine meadows are called tundra from a Russian word meaning "land of no trees."

"As children, and if we're lucky as adults, we know what it is to be 'at play in the fields of the lord.' We know what it is to be in the presence of what is not human, not self, and to respond from the gut, as intact beings, to the oceanic and subtly fused logos we shall never name. We learn the fundamentals of reverence and humility in the face of beauty, the power and scale of life and death. We learn to move, to think with this mind." In this brief quote from Casey Walker we can experience the power of the *tan tien*, the lower brain.

Form 39 – Single Whip.

"Like a Taoist sage, geneticist Barbara Mc Clintock's attitude is ironic. Both reductionist and holist, she strives to get to the bottom of things which she is aware have no bottom. In her sense of the whole…she revels in the uncertainties, interrelationships, and mutual dependencies that pervade nature… . All these things were happening and we didn't see it."

from *Turbulent Mirror* on Chaos Theory by J. Briggs & F. Peat

In both this photo and the next two Jodi does three of the forms most specifically involved with self defense; but also high in chi energy. The word tiger means energy in Chinese thought.

Behind her is the High Divide. Rapidly moving clouds flow over the deep green tundra. Hit a Tiger at Left flows invisibly into the next movement. Yin turns into yang and on into yin as sun and clouds and the heavens and the green tundra of earth move and change.

Form 51 – Hit a Tiger at Left. The two fists make a half circle and then with no bodily change swing the other way and make a half circle for Hit a Tiger at Right. The turning action is on the heels of the feet; the body remains the same. This form helps the entire back area and the knees and ankles to be more elastic as well as generate chi energy.

" Winter! Avalanches poured off the cliffs,
sometimes bringing death to animals and humans.
Summer! Now, deeply piled snow, under the cliffs,
slowly melting, giving life. "

Jodi flows into the form, Hit a Tiger at Right, with the bright sun on her right side and her fist upraised toward the distant snow highlighted by the sun. Flowers flow below her, flourishing from the meltwater, and clouds are scudding by above her. Tiny white alpine phlox and moss campion hug the ground and blossom unseen in the distance on the wind-scoured tundra above her and on the far distant cliffs there's left-over avalanche snow.

American bistort, red paintbrush and larkspur blooming at her feet make a lush oasis beneath still another cliff band in front of her.

The wild forces of nature – summer and winter – are here. It's far wilder and far more complex than we can know. Such glimpses of nature's power gives the lie to the modern idea of nature controlled by human thought, which is modern science in its reductionist nightmare.

"Against this trend rises the young science of chaos, wholeness, and change – a new insistence on the interrelationships of things, an awareness of the essential unpredictableness of nature and of the uncertainties of our scientific descriptions" (J. Briggs and F. Peat). This "new" science of chaos, of course, is the ancient Taoist way of looking at things. By moving in the ancient Chinese way of Tai Chi we begin to learn to really "see" nature and thus find our way out of the trap of rational thinking.

Form 52 – Hit a Tiger at Right.

*" A south wind fragrant with blue
distance
luffs my hair... "*
Robert MacLean

Between yin and yang, Jodi has a lush, flower-filled meadow before her and seemingly barren, wind-scoured ground behind her. Strike Both Ears brings chi energy to the upper body and in the next breath sends it down to the *tan tien*. The two fists make a circular form which encloses all the energy circulating through her body, unifying all parts so that the ground she is standing on manifests in her hands.

She moves within the yang of the bright flowers before her and the approaching yin cloud shadow behind her.

It's not the things that are related through Jodi's actions here but "the relationship" itself which matters. We can't possibly count all the things – the tiny, hidden flowers on the seemingly barren wind-swept tundra, the myriads of flowers just before her, the moving clouds above her, the rocks, and the the cliffs – but if she is in relationship to all that, we are not limited by the narrowly rational counting and itemizing of each separate thing.

Gregory Bateson says that if you approach the natural world from the point of view of relationships, "You will meet with *beauty* and *ugliness*." He admits it is revolutionary "to assert, as a scientist, that matters of beauty are really highly formal, very real, and crucial to the entire political and ethical system in which we live… ." Continuing, he says that the "viewing of the world in terms of things is a distortion supported by language, and that the correct view of the world is in terms of the dynamic relations which are the governors of growth." He ends with this startling statement, the last sentence of his last book, *A Sacred Unity* and hence his last words to us:

"I believe that perhaps the monstrous atomistic pathology at the individual level, at the family level, at the national level and the international level – the pathology of wrong thinking in which we all live – can only in the end be corrected by an enormous discovery of those relations in nature which make up the beauty of nature."

Form 54 – Strike Opponent's Ears with Both Fists.

As Jodi begins the move, Apparent Close Up, she has completed a back hand push and her left hand is now below. Her right hand seems to be attacking, moving forward, but actually at this moment there is a "stillness" as she experiences all the beauty of the myriad flowers, the pure, clear air, the chi energy from all around her, before the next part of the move.

The psychologist James Hillman tells us of the importance of beauty: "Nothing so moves the soul as an aesthetic leap of the heart." Yet our culture generally ignores beauty. Hillman traces this pathology back to its puritan origins when he says: "Puritanism...is the structural fiber of America… we are *supposed* to be sensually numb. That is the fundamental nature of puritan goodness. We are numb because we are anaesthetized, without aesthetics, aesthetically unconscious, beauty repressed. Just look at our land – this continent's astonishing beauty – and then look at what we immigrants, Bibles in hand, priests and preachers in tow, have done to it…as a people we are void of beauty and devoted to ugliness."

The beauty of this flower-filled meadow is constantly renewed each year by the avalanches which crash down from the cliffs above. They hit so hard that the resulting wind wave rises high and gently drops layer after layer of snow into this area. The large snowbanks which result melt slowly along their edges throughout the summer, providing plenty of water which soaks gently into the ground. This continuous source of water, along with the power of a high altitude sun, produces the true wealth of abundant life.

Form 59 – Apparent Close Up.

Apparent Close Up

*"There's life here and we're being watched
from below where the pines think
or by what we call air
what surrounds us is waiting
boulders, startled grass, frozen water
the infinitesimal immensity of the reciprocal
private beauty of what functions through us."*

J. B. Bryan

Jodi now fully opens her right hand and draws in all this wealth of beauty around her. In reciprocal relationship, the plants give oxygen to her and in return she breathes out carbon dioxide for the plants. Chi energy circulates all through her. Apparent Close Up comes just before the concluding move, Return to Mountain, which occurs at the end of each of the three sections in Tai Chi.

Jodi is surrounded by the splendor of the high altitude meadow in bloom.

Yet, as James Hillman tells us, "our culture just can't accept aesthetics as essential to the daily round." He continues by saying, "But for me, the greatest moral choice we can make today, if we are truly concerned with the oppressed and stressed lives of our clients' souls, is to sharpen their sense of beauty…. Deep ecology begins in our aesthetic responses."

Form 59 – Apparent Close Up tones the spinal nerves and abdominal organs. For this form the feet remain stationary but the body moves back, drawing in chi energy.

> *Flowers and bushes*
> *reflected*
> *played by the gentle breeze into ripples of light.*

For this form we have come down from the brief summer of the high alpine tundra to the lower valley. Ages ago an enormous rock fell from the cliffs above and rolled to a stop with its flat side up, providing a perfectly flat, smooth rock surface for Tai Chi. There's no water flowing into the pond. Just above the pond is a talus slope made up of all the rocks falling from the steep cliffs above, which extend all the way up to the top of Galena Mountain, 13,278 ft. high. Seemingly there is no source of water anywhere; but actually it wells up from deep within the mountain itself and surfaces here at 9600 ft. just above the valley floor.

In Needle at Sea Bottom, Jodi bends her knees and drops down her right hand to the "sea of breath", her *tan tien*. Her other hand pushes down toward the solid rock surface. Her back is straight so she can look ahead.

The *tan tien*, or in Japanese, the *hara*, is succinctly described by Richard Pilgrim "as the seat or source of psychic/spiritual energy and force (in the lower abdominal area); to fulfill or to live based in *hara* is to live authentically, holistically, integratively." This is to follow nature's way, as the Taoists say. Pilgrim continues his explanation of the importance of the *hara* by quoting from Durkheim: "It is a liberation from the domination of an 'I', an anchoring in the ground of Being, a self which manifests Being and a transformation, expansion, deepening and intensifying of the whole personality." To express this unity with nature in a poetic way, Pilgrim refers to the famous Japanese poet, Basho, who used the word, *fuga* to describe the sense of absolute unity with nature. Explaining the spirit of *fuga*, Basho wrote that "he who cherishes it accepts Nature and becomes a friend of the four seasons. Whatever objects he sees are referred to the flowers: whatever thoughts he conceives are related to the moon."

Form 34 – Needle at Sea Bottom increases the flow of chi in the spinal cord and benefits the joints of the knees. In the self defense aspect, the right hand extends down, fingers lined up to resemble a needle. A sudden drop in the knees and extending this hand can pressure the "Sea Bottom" point in acupuncture on the foot of the opponent.

> *Sun pulsating on top of the water*
> *The pond*
> *vibrates*
> *cauldron of breathing wiggling being born screwing*
> *being dead creatures.*
> Robert MacLean

Jodi rises up from the rock into the next form, Fan Through the Back. She turns her foot in, one hand at her chest and the other at her forehead. Then she spins around on this foot. As she turns, her arms move apart like an opening fan and she ends up facing the opposite direction. Her entire body is balancing on one foot – that slender bundle of bone and tendons and muscle where all the acupuncture points for the internal organs crisscross on the sole. The tendons effortlessly accomplish this move for her.

Below the rock are two stumps. These aspen were long ago chiseled off by beavers as part of the construction of their dam, which retains the upwelling water, creating this small pond. The water wells up out of the depths of Galena Mountain but without the beavers it would trickle away down into Cunningham Creek, lost amid the jumble of loose talus rock. But the beavers' work safely contains the water in this small area, creating an oasis of life in the midst of the rocks. There is a balancing of yin and yang forces with the yin of the cold water and the dark side of the rock and the yang of the bright sun as it rises over the mountain, glinting off the top surface of the rock and illuminating Jodi's feet in conforming contact with the rock.

Form 35 – Fan Through the Back. In this form one can feel the arms connect across the back, expanding the lungs at the back. We seldom remember that our lungs are capable of expanding the ribs in the back as well as the front. Through Tai Chi the lungs regain this ability, which they had in childhood.

" Clouds flowing above
Clouds flowing below "

Jodi has just completed the Cloud Hands series, which comes after Fan Through the Back. She turns around with the Single Whip form. As her hand moves across her body, the palm turns out, gathering chi energy from the wrist tendon as she takes in more of the beauty in this place.

We are now looking at her from the opposite side of this impressive rock. In the ancient Shinto religion of Japan, the *Kami* (the Power) "chose its residence" – usually a stone, a tree or a flower or a pond. Here we have all these different Kamis together in one small area. The "residence" was where the human experienced the presence of the Kami.

The aesthetic power of this combination of beauty in such a small area evokes the feeling of reverence while doing Tai Chi. The world is felt in a deeper way and this connection between all the life around and her moving body creates the sacred in this place.

The yin and yang continually change around her as the clouds move across and reflect in the pond. The yang of the sun is on the side of the rock and on Jodi while the yin of the dark cloud shadow is on the mountain. The yin of the dark shadow and the yang of Jodi's white tunic are reflected in the water.

Form 41 – Single Whip. Jodi's outstretched left arm is hidden behind her body.

> *He danced the moor...He danced the mist and the sky.*
> *He danced all the odours and all that he saw, and all that*
> *touched his eyes, his ears, his nostrils, and his skin. He danced*
> *the world that had thus entered his being.*
> Jean Giono

Jodi begins the kicks part of Section II with Separation of Right Foot, followed by Separation of Left Foot and then a spin around with still another kick. The knee joint must be kept slightly bent for these kicks.

This poetic quote from Giono about the deer dancing in the meadow shows us the intensity of mammalian interaction with the surrounding environment. Although we humans are mammals, too, we have lost much of this awareness, but through Tai Chi we can regain more use of our senses.

For many years Alan Drengson has put out the Canadian environmental magazine, *The Trumpeter*. He does Aikido, which is based on Tai Chi, but was developed in Japan in the twentieth century. He writes about how these techniques… "harmonize movement and coordinate breathing." He continues, "Our energy is focused on more complete awareness through movement in harmony with the place we are in… . when we feel unified in this way, our bodies lose their heaviness. We feel radiant. We are unified with the wild energies of the natural world… . Each human being, no matter how civilized or domesticated, tamed, subdued, or enslaved still has some wildness within."

Wildness lies deep within us, in our lower brain, the *tan tien*.

Form 43 – Separation of Right Foot strengthens the legs and balances the torso.

Separation of Right Foot

In the Manyoshu (Collection of Myriad Leaves), the oldest anthology of Japanese poems, many poets sang to and about rivers, oceans, celestial and atmospheric phenomena, animals, birds, insects, and flowers as living beings possessing intimate relations with men and women. Indeed, to them 'nature is man's friend and companion and there still exists a sense of mutual sympathy' based on the appreciative awareness of the mutual participation that evokes reverence and affection on both sides.

Joseph Kitagawa summing up Manyoshu poets

Jodi does the final part of the three kicks. After spinning around from the Separation of Right and Left Foot she kicks out with her sole. She faces the opposite direction and so looks directly up the scree slope to the high cliffs above.

With the continually moving clouds, yin and yang change. The yin of the dark water has grown larger while the yellow blossoms of the shrubby cinquefoil have grown brighter and thus more yang.

Our town of Silverton lies in the valley just beyond the left ridge.

Form 45 – Turn and Kick with Sole.

Turn and kick with Sole

> *I rest on the piled-up heights and tread the roots of the clouds.*
> *Hsieh Ling-yun*

We've moved a short distance above the small pond to take advantage of the curve on the old mining road to Stony Pass. This provides a flat space among the towering cliffs.

Here Jodi does Cloud Hands, moving as effortlessly as the billowing clouds rising over the ridge behind her.

The wind moving the clouds also moves through the hollows of the cliffs. Chuang Tzu calls this "piping." Kuang Ming-Wu explains: "Piping comes when two non-beings meet, hollows in things and the blowing wind." Chuang Tzu says: "Gentle wind, then a small chorus; whirling wind, then a huge chorus." By "selflessly listening," Wu tells us, "We discern three pipings – the piping of men, of earth, and of heaven… . Three pipings are both distinct and interactive. The piping of men is inspired by, as it interacts with, the piping of their surroundings, the piping of earth. And both pipings reveal their root, the piping of heaven, which manifests itself only in them. The Muses stir up nature into 'beings' of musical resonance, to which human beings respond by singing with it in their daily ongoings, and by sometimes composing music out of its inspiration.

Form 76 – Wave Hands Like Clouds. See the previous series of Cloud Hands photos, Forms 28 to 30, for more about Jodi's movements in this form.

" The rocks are ringing..."
Paiute chant

The sky is completely inhabited by immense clouds, the wind carries them along and animates them with a great life. Jodi moves with the wind.

Clouds moving, Jodi moving, her tunic blowing, rocks ringing in the wind: all interacting. Kuang Ming Wu says: "This leads us to look into reciprocity among things, the cosmic, fugal chorus of earthly and human pipings, which Chuang Tzu described... . Music or piping is an organized group of sounds, a structured non-being that is not nothing. And piping is of three levels, each closely interrelated to the other two; we see in one the other two. The world is a mutuality of pipings of cosmic-and-individual life. To discern and live it is joy; to violate it in self-assertion is confusion and suffering."

Form 76 – Wave Hands Like Clouds.

> *"...up high in the mountains where stone and sky joined, the light's common ground."*
> Harry Middleton

Jodi completes the third movement of Cloud Hands. The wind is stronger, the sound in the rocks louder, and the light clearer.

Kuang Ming-Wu leads us still deeper into the three pipings when he writes: " 'Music' is piped forth from a hollow through a nothing-power, the wind. The 'music' comes out of the meeting and resonance among things that are really nothings. Earthly piping is resonance among such things (*wu*): human piping is thinking and debating about such things, a resonance with such thing-resonance (*lun*). Heavenly piping is what begins and arranges all this (*ch'i*), the yet-to-begin to yet-to-begin all these. This is the cosmic music, three levels of polyphonic fugue, produced in the meeting of wind with hollows, resonance among nothings.

"Resonance requires at least two things for it to come about. Things arise by reciprocal interaction."

Quoting Chuang Tzu directly:

"The winding of recesses of mountains, forests; hundreds of spans of huge trees, their hollows and openings…

Huge understanding widens, widens…"

Form 76 – Wave Hands Like Clouds.

> *A large part of Balinese behavior is based upon paradigms of balance and of the interaction between the moving human body and the gravitational field in which it must move.*
>
> Gregory Bateson

Jodi's balance is rooted deep into the earth as she does Golden Cock Stands on One Leg She stands firm and unwaveringly on the edge of the precipice.

In both China and Japan, the cock symbolizes high esteem and in China cocks were kept at Imperial courts. The silhouette of the bird was much admired and many artists painted the cock. In China the cock with peonies was a symbol for spring and also for a happy life.

Cock fighting was a very important social and in some cases religious activity in much of Southeastern Asia, including Bali.

The cock, also called the rooster, keeps a vigilant eye on his hens – both to protect them from harm and to keep other roosters away. He often stands on one leg, both for resting and for quick movement in case something attacks his hens.

Form 79 – Golden Cock Stands on One Leg (right). This form generates chi in the spinal column and the tai tien. It also improves stability and balance for all the other forms used in Tai Chi.

Golden Cock Stand on One Leg

> *Yin spruce, shadowed by the clouds*
> *marching down the precipice*
> *Yang aspen*
> *fluttering in the sun*

Jodi stands on her left leg, balanced between yin of the dark trees and yang of the aspen and between the yang of the bright sun-lit rock of the cliffs and the distant mountain and the yin of the dark depths of the precipice below. Yin and yang are always changing but she remains balanced.

An ancient legend tells of the Emperor Yao, "who with great wisdom and skillful foreign policy managed to maintain peace in his empire" for many years. There was a huge gong hanging at the gate of the imperial palace which was used to summon soldiers to battle. It was never struck during Yao's reign because he kept the peace so well. Since it was never disturbed it provided good shelter for a rooster and his hens: thus the rooster became a symbol of peace in China.

In Japan where cock fighting was popular the rooster became the symbol for martial strength as well as prestige. It was often used in the design of "mons", the Japanese crests for nobles.

Form 80 – Golden Cock Stands on One Leg (L).

Golden Cock Stand on One Leg

" As the sun pours like honey through the ponderosa pine
You're living every moment as if you just arrived
Cause you know what it means to be alive. "

Walking Jim Stoltz

It's late summer. We move down to the lower edge of the Alpine zone to this beautiful old growth ponderosa. We are overcome by the beauty and serenity and filled with gratitude that there are still a few of these glorious old trees left. Jodi sits at the foot of the great tree, absorbing ponderosa through all her senses before beginning Tai Chi.

This area still has the open park-like aspect of a true ponderosa forest. Few of these areas are left anywhere in the west. Most of the ponderosa were heavily logged at the beginning of this century because they were easily accessible and produced excellent wood for buildings, mining timbers and railroad ties.

Before the massive destruction of the old growth, the ponderosa naturally grew widely spaced as a result of frequent and low intensity fires, which were once a natural part of the ecosystem throughout the West. Sugar pine and ponderosa are the biggest of all the pines.

The sun-warmed bark has a unique smell. Some say vanilla; others say butterscotch. Whatever, it's unique to ponderosa and gives one a peaceful, relaxed feeling as soon as you walk among the trees.

The number 'three' (san) is one of the favorites of the Chinese.
It has three implications:
(1) 'Three' expresses the multiplicity of...an object, and
multiplicity in turn implies abundance and inexhaustibility.
(2) Three' expresses an intensity of meaning...
'three trees' means a forest...
(3) 'Three' is the way of heaven, earth, and man.
Although usually spatial, 'three' is used processively by
Taoism and in the **Book of Changes,** *with all the preceding*
implications of abundance and intensity. Without explicitly
treating 'three', Chuang Tzu often resorts to 'three' to express the
processive dynamism of growth into sageliness...
Kuang-Ming Wu

Jodi raises her arm in the Slanting Flying form in a gesture of homage to the "great ones". In this form the arms imitate the spreading wings of a flying bird.

Darwin showed us that all individual organisms are connected through time but, as Lynn Margulis explains: "Vernadsky showed us that organisms are not only connected through time but also through space. The carbon dioxide we exhale as a waste product becomes the life-giving force for a plant; in turn the oxygen waste of a plant gives us life. This exchange of gas is what the word *spirit* means. Spirituality is essentially the act of breathing. But the connection doesn't stop at the exchange of gases in the atmosphere. We are also physically connected, and you can see this everywhere you look. Think of the protists that live in the hind-gut of the termite, or the fungi that live in the rootstock of trees and plants. The birds that flitter from tree to tree transport fungi spores throughout the environment. Their droppings host a community of insects and microorganisms. When rain falls on the droppings, spores are splashed back up on the tree, creating pockets for life to begin to grow again. This interdependence is an inexorable fact of life. As Vernadsky said, without this interdependence, no organism can hope to survive."

Form 30 – Slanting Flying.

Slanting Flying

"We are left in awe by the nobility of a tree, its eternal patience, its suffering caused by man and sometimes by nature, its witness to thousands of years of earth's history, its creation of fabulous beauty. It does nothing but good, with its prodigious ability to serve, it gives off its bounty of oxygen while absorbing gases harmful to other living beings.... Its branches shade and protect us. And finally when the time and weather bring it down, its body offers timber for our houses and boards for our furniture. The tree lives on."*

George Nakashima

Jodi is just completing the form, Stork Cools Its Wings. This movement also expresses her wonder at the power of the tree. In the beginning of Stork Cools Its Wings, she has drawn in the chi energy through her finger tips and the tendons in her arms and wrists, breathing it in down through her body. Now, in extending her arm up she breathes out. Chi energy flows all through her body and up her arm and her breath gives carbon dioxide to the tree in a continuous interchange, while her feet are firmly rooted in the ground.

Form 32 – Stork Cools Its Wings.

> *I have noticed in my life that all men have a liking for some special animal, or plant, or spot of earth. If men would pay more attention to these preferences and seek what is best to do in order to make themselves worthy of that toward which they are so attracted, they might have dreams which would purify their lives.*
>
> Brave Buffalo, Sioux Medicine man, born in 1911 on the Standing Rock Reservation.

Standing very near the powerful ponderosa, Jodi does Hit a Tiger At Right. Remember "tiger" refers to energy in Tai Chi. Her hand circles toward the tree, gathering chi energy and continues the circle by moving toward her body. Her left arm is down at her tan tien, focusing chi energy there.

Form 52 – Hit a Tiger At Right. In the self-defense aspect, the fist strikes high on the opponent, hitting the temple, a very disabling blow. See photos 36 and 37 for more about the movements in the "Hit a Tiger" forms.

Hit Tiger At Right

> *"To fill the pattern as it is, fill and grow*
> *with natural root, stem, leaves...*
> *accept the seasons as they fill and flow."*
>
> Robert MacLean

Doing Snake Creeps Down, Jodi drops close to the root of the great tree. These roots bring up nourishment from deep within the earth. Awareness of the hundreds of years of life of this tree gives us a deep sense of place, an awareness of the flow of time and a feeling of how these deep roots nourish us with the beauty and majesty of such a tree.

"Man's love for natural colors, patterns and harmonies, his preference for forest-grassland ecotones which he recreates wherever he settles, even in drastically different landscapes, must be the result (at least to a very large degree) of Darwinian natural selection through eons of mammalian and anthropoid evolutionary time... . Our eyes and ears, noses, brain and bodies have all been shaped by nature. Would it not then be incredible indeed, if savannas and forest groves, flowers and animals, the multiplicity of environmental components to which our bodies were originally shaped, were not, at the very least, still important to us?" (Hugh Iltis)

Form 78 – Snake Creeps Down. See the previous series of this form in photos 31 to 33.

> ❝*Of all pines, this one gives forth the finest music to the winds.*❞
> *John Muir on the Ponderosa Pine*

In the golden light of late afternoon sun, Jodi completes the second section of Tai Chi with Apparent Close Up. She has completed the punch by the wrist and is now drawing all the accumulated chi into her body before turning around and finishing with Embrace Tiger, Return to Mountain, the concluding form for each section of Tai Chi.

Seeing Jodi move within this grassy forest grove gives us a longing to be there. Paul Shepard tells us that the origins of human beings began in a forest/grassland ecotone back in the Pleistocene era. Shepard continues: "No one, it is said, can go back to the Pleistocene… . But that is irrelevant. Having never left our genome and its authority, we have never left the past, which is part of ourselves, and have only to bring the Pleistocene to us. Regardless of the lines drawn to end that period by geologists and archaeologists, we remain 'in' it. Fortunately it is not only a Thing or a Place, or a Time, but a mosaic lifeway, a living embroidery. We continue to share the world with most of the families of plants and animals who were also part of it."

Shepard points out that a culture is "an assemblage, not a monolith. The omnivorous mode and small-scale community of human life is not a mono anything – monotheism, monogamy, monopoly, or monotony." He makes it clear that it is possible to once again live in the optimum human culture. "The Pleistocene is constructible in terms of its ontogenetic, economic, social, ecological, and cosmological characteristics." And we can regain that. He goes on to say that we do not have to continue to "play in a world of virtual reality, we can once again *live* in actual places."

Paul Shepard wrote these inspiring words in his last book, *Traces of an Omnivore*, published before he died in July 1996. In this essay he distilled a lifetime of studying humans – both their origins and how they are part of the natural world.

This last photo of summer gives us the feeling, deep within us, of how it feels to be fully human, moving within the natural world.

Form 59 – Apparent Close Up.

Autumn

" Now, what of that celestial movement which decrees the
succession of those mysterious moods of the Earth Being we call
The Seasons? That movement gives us a new sense of Land Sky
Embodiment, ever deepening through the spiral of the Seasons. "
Frederick Adams

Here in Silverton, the aspen leaves turn golden and the clear light of the blue sky is at its best. It is all warm and golden and a kind of hush lies over everything. There seems to be a stillness of balance between the end of summer and the beginning of winter. In traditional agricultural countries of the more temperate zones it was the time of gathering in of the harvest and thus a giving thanks time.

In ancient traditional eras, the Chinese celebrated certain times of the year when the earth is most yin or most yang. One of these is the Full Moon Festival in September, when summer heat gives place to autumn coolness. This full moon is considered the time when the female or yin principle begins to take over the upper hand in Nature. Concerning this full moon, the Chinese say: "At no other time is she so bright and brilliant. Then, and then only, the Chinese say, 'she is perfectly round'." The feast is "usually at midnight – the hour when the moon illumines the highest palaces. General festivities continue for three days. The evenings are devoted to moon-viewing parties which date from the time of Emperor Wu Ti (100 BC)."

There are two different approaches to autumn – one a battle with bad influences or devils and one a calm, peaceful balance. Autumn equinox is the main festival day of this season: it is a day of balancing all the forces within and without, while Hallowe'en partakes much more of the aspects of encountering "darkness" without and within the human. At the autumn equinox we have equal day and equal night, which is a balancing of the relationship between earth and sun.

The aspen "blazes, scattering leafsparks, its sensitive nerves first to convey the season's summons...
Robert MacLean

Our early autumn weather is unsettled here in the San Juan Mountains but later, true autumn arrives and we have day after day of glorious sun and yellow aspen. One early autumn afternoon of a stormy day it finally clears a bit and a few bright yellow leaves draw us up to a small hill just above town.

During the season of autumn we do only the forms for the final section, Section Three of Tai Chi. Jodi does Step Back and Repulse Monkey, moving backward through the aspen, amongst a scattering of glowing yellow leaves. Her right hand drops low, palm facing up and then her arm circles around and up and moves past her right ear, with the palm facing down toward the earth. Moving out past her head her palm turns up facing forward. Her left hand is lowered to her hip level, palm facing up.

Her left hand circles around in the same way as the right hand and arm circled before. These movements are continued while Jodi steps backward. Her arms moving, like alternate turning wheels, circulate chi energy throughout her entire body.

Form 81 – In Step Back and Repulse Monkey extra chi energy is generated as the hand moves from its position parallel to the earth and then turns upward, stretching the wrist tendon. The self defense aspect of this form is based on the idea of holding up one hand to repulse an approaching monkey and retreating away at the same time while keeping the other hand ready for attack at the appropriate moment.

"...a mind obeying and at one with nature throughout the four seasons..."
Basho

Jodi has stepped back again and she finds herself moving beneath an entire branch of golden leaves glistening in the sunlight.

Cherry blossoms have been considered *kami* (sacred) for hundreds of years in Japan. Special pilgrimages are made to view them and all the famous Japanese poets of the past have written about them. The twelfth century poet, Saigyo wrote of the "saving power of nature". He found it often when he was "united with the moon...when he gave...his body to the safekeeping of a pine tree, and when his heart and mind were 'taken' by the blossoms of spring." La Fleur explains further: "The action involved is always one of giving, yielding, and surrendering – as if it is the Absolute to which he is giving himself."

The golden aspen of autumn affect us in the same way. After visiting aspen in a "sacred manner" for a couple of years, it's enough just to walk into the grove and the sacred feeling overpowers one and a hush comes over the world.

This experience grows deeper and deeper with each passing year. The aspen tree has helped me understand reciprocal appropriation. The aspen does not greedily hang onto its leaves, which it has spent all summer producing from the light of the sun, the water from the sky and the nutrients which its roots draw up from the earth. Instead, at the culmination of their growth in autumn, the leaves become a glory of gold and fly off to enrich the soil below. Doing Tai Chi midst the golden aspen teaches us "the Way" of giving and yielding instead of forcing or demanding.

Form 81 – Step Back and Repulse Monkey (left).

> *The mountain soars in majesty to heaven*
> *Through the thousandfold white clouds.*
>
> Manyoshu

Suddenly Jodi "steps back" into winter. As she moves out of the golden aspen, the wildness of newly fallen snow looms in the distance on a sunlit peak. Spring and autumn, transitional times, are unsure and unpredictable but with the Tao, utterly natural. Through Tai Chi we learn to move in balance with continual change.

N. J. Girardot gives us a concise explanation of the importance of the relationship between the Tao and transitional times when he writes: "Tao, as the source and ground of nature, constantly 'returns' to the conditions of the Beginning in the sense of a periodic reiteration of the cosmogony. This *creatio continua* of many constant interrelated 'transitional moments' (lunar, solar, seasonal, diurnal, bodily, psychic, etc.) is the essential life principle of Tao in the world. The renewal of man and society depends on an emulation of this 'way'. The continual rhythm of 'beginning and return' is both the macrocosmic life of Tao in nature and the microcosmic true life of man."

Form 81 – In the form, Step Back and Repulse Monkey, we clearly see "Circular power returning into itself in the power of regeneration," as Bruce Wilshire explains it.

Step Back and Repulse Monkey

> *"...making the spring and autumn with the heaven and earth."*
> *Chuang Tzu*

Jodi does Slanting Flying based on how a bird slants its wings while turning in flight. She moves into this form, stretching from her spine. She is making the spring and autumn with the heaven and earth as she goes along with her spinal artery.

Chuang Tzu says: "…we had better go-along-with the spinal-artery of energy, with which we make our constant passage. With it we can maintain our body-and-life; with it we can keep our life whole."

Chuang Tzu then tells the story of the cook who cut up the oxen so skillfully that his knife never needed sharpening. The Ruler wonders how can there be such skill. Kuang Ming Wu explains for us: "All this is joy and expertise; and it is natural…. Nature is rhythmical – in space and in season, at the right spot and time. To find and dwell in the spatio-temporal rightness is to be natural, to be an expert. No wonder the Lord is delighted. It is the delightful expertise of undoing the ox of things."

The movement of the cook's knife remind the Ruler of two pieces of ancient Chinese music: the dance of the Mulberry Forest and the music of Ching Shou. Wu points out that these two pieces of music are "unmistakably those of the spring, the rain, and the rising of life with the sun." But the knife is that of "autumnal slaughter, the opposite of the spring of life. Here then life and death are joined in the dance – of life! The butcher's expertise is the skill that joins life and death, the spring and the autumn in the dance that rises with the rain and the sun." He continues: "In sum the phrase, "*i* (heaven-earth) *wei* (spring-autumn)" is at once obvious and obscure, personal and cosmic, joyous and natural."

Form 82 – Slanting Flying.

> *The sky is completely inhabited by immense clouds. The wind carries them along, and pushes them and animates them with a great life.*

Jodi does Cloud Hands, her feet rooted on the rock while she faces the wide, cloud-filled sky as she turns around her spine. The emptiness of the spinal artery allows the chi to flow through her. In a similar manner the seemingly empty clouds nourish the earth with water.

There seems to be nothing physical in a cloud. One can pass right through it while climbing a mountain or fly through it in a plane, but the emptiness of the cloud becomes rain as it falls down to the earth.

"The image of spinal artery can be helpful," says Chuang Tzu. "Artery is an empty tube that carries, or rather, lets through, the flow of energy whether in the form of blood, nerves, or chi the breathing energy, in short, the energy of life. Such vital energy throbs and thrusts itself everywhere like a flood. What regulates and makes it a particular living being (such as a man, or an ox) is that *tu*, that vital emptiness which lets through the energy of life in a particular manner." Summing up, Kuang-Ming Wu says: "*Tu* is the vital emptiness that lets through and lets be."

It is necessary to be empty and loosened to become oneself. Wu continues: "And to go being-loosened is thereby to loosen others as well. The cook becomes thickless as the knife enters the inner space of the ox. He lets the spirit that pervades the universe go through him, that is, loosen him, and thereby loosens the ox."

The spine is at the center of our back, invisible but it is this spine that supports us. "We must be *on* it, to become as we are," Wu succinctly explains. "To stay on in *tu* and flow with the concrete vicissitudes (dealing with an ox, the wild environment, politics, life-years) is the way to become free in whatever interchange one must undergo (*hua*); we see here an application of two key notions (*fen* and *hua*)."

Back in his commentary on Chapter Two of the Chuang Tzu, "Things, Theories – Sorting Themselves Out", Wu told us that these two qualities "distinct identities (*yu fen*) obtained in their interchanges (*wu hua*) – make up the world."

Form 92 – Wave Hands Like Clouds.

" Sun flashed on trembling leaves."

There's a last glimmer of sun on the distant aspen, touched with gold, and a new rain shower, moving up the valley. Jodi continues Cloud Hands, turning round her spine, hands drifting down as the distant aspen leaves drift down. Her feet effortlessly conform to the contour of the rock.

Chuang Tzu says of the "true men" of ancient times: "Their breathing was calm and deep. They used to breathe with their heels." Izutsu continues: "This indicates the incomparable depth and tranquillity of their respiration. The vital energy contained in the inhaled air is made to circulate all through the body, in such a way that one is left with the impression as if the breathing naturally welled up from the heels."

Echoing Chuang Tzu's words about the concept of *tu*, Bruce Wilshire, a modern philosopher writes: "Through opening to the world, the world opens to us. As if one were a wise child and the universe a mother, there is interdependency. The Mother turns us gently when we are bent on rushing over the edge. The test of an art of life and its truth is whether it allows circular power to return fluently into itself through ourselves."

Form 92 – Wave Hands Like Clouds. In his commentary on Chapter Three of the Chuang Tzu, Kuang Ming-Wu tells us of the effortlessness and emptiness when one stays on in the state of *tu*. He sums up by saying: "The resemblance of this movement to that of Tai Chi Chuan, a Chinese martial art, is uncanny."

Wave Hands Like Clouds

*" Whirling, twirling autumn leaves
shower gold upon the ground. "*

After Cloud Hands, Jodi goes into the final moves of Tai Chi but the rain shower has arrived, darkening everything. We wait while it moves on by. The sun flashes out for a moment as she does Shoot Tiger with Bow.

Remember tiger means energy in Chinese thought. She extends her energy and draws in the surrounding chi energy of the trees and the rain.

Form 104 – Shoot Tiger with Bow.

Shoot Tiger with Bow

> *D. H. Lawrence emphasized the great nerve center which "lies in the middle front of the abdomen, beneath the navel." He once told Rhys Davies, 'When you have come to a decision, whatever your mental calculations tell you, go by what you feel here.' Davies explains, 'With his quick intent gesture he placed his hands over and around his belly - "go by that, what you feel deep in you, not by what your head tells you".' Lady Asquith wrote that it seemed to her that Lawrence thought 'with his solar plexus rather than with his brain.'*

Jodi begins Apparent Close Up and is just completing the final push of that form when the lowering black clouds above us let loose and we run for shelter in the car, which is parked just below us on the dirt road.

In this final push Jodi breathes deeply into the tan tien. This is followed by the final form, Embrace Tiger Return to Mountain but the rain has begun so we must leave, planning to do more of the forms in Section III another day.

While in Chinese this important "lower brain" is called tan tien, in Japanese it is called the *hara*. Fosco Maraini beautifully describes the actions of this "lower brain". He writes that it frees "the mind of the tyranny of reason, with its pernicious distinctions between the self and the non-self, between mind and matter, between gods and the world." Again, writing of the *hara*, he states that it provides the "bridge between the self and the non-self which reason is unable to provide."

Maraini is an Italian who went to Japan to study the primitives of Japan, the Ainu, before World War II, fell in love with the country and stayed. We have here the elegantly stated testimony of two European authors on the power of deep breathing into the *tan tien* or *hara*.

Form 107 – Apparent Close Up.

There's a break in the weather and we travel down to lower Lime Creek on the southern edge of San Juan County. Here Jodi parts Wild Horse's Mane while moving through the golden aspen. This movement derives from the action of separating the horse's mane lovingly. The back of one hand separates one part of the mane while the palm of the other hand smooths the rest of the mane. When a horse is running free, every time it turns, the mane parts.

In ancient China the horse was honored; not broken to use as a work horse or to be ridden in battle. The Chinese did have chariots pulled by horses but armed invaders from Central Asia came on horseback which made it much easier for manoeuvering. Thus these skilled horsemen were able successfully to invade China on numerous occasions.

Form 63 – Partition of Wild Horse's Mane (Right). This form generates very strong chi energy. As the hands are separated you feel the chi on one side of the spine and, at the same time, you feel the chi at the opposite side of the spine as the arms open and close.

Partition of Wild
Horse's Mane

" Aspen's trembling leaves
flickering yellow
Sailing down...down... "

Jodi continues moving through unfolding beauty. In the far distance looms Twilight Peak, appearing through the fog.

In one of the her last talks, shortly before she died, Rachel Carson told a meeting of nearly a thousand women journalists: "I am not afraid of being thought a sentimentalist when I stand here tonight and tell you that I believe natural beauty has a necessary place in the spiritual development of any individual or any society."

Form 64 – Partition of Wild Horse's Mane (Right).

> *Sun flashes on fluttering leaves*
> *midst lingering green*
> *distant white of coming winter*

Jodi weaves the world about her as she turns through the four directions of Fair Lady at Shuttles. Raising her sun-filled hands she begins the weaving, facing towering Twilight Peak.

In the mythology of many different cultures including the ancient Chinese culture, the Japanese culture and the Navajo tribe, a sacred woman weaves their world.

Paul Shepard explains that the way of the sacred is "not a leap from this world to the other but a leap like the shuttle of a loom, finding and informing rather than departing" from this world.

There is a regular, orderly, disciplined, binding acitivty which is obvious in the smooth operation of a loom. This almost hypnotic effect of a loom being worked provides a metaphor for many cultures' myths of both time and space in their cosmos.

Form 69 – Fair Lady Works at Shuttles (1). Fair Lady involves a diagonal turning into the four corners in counter-clockwise order. It's an intricate form but when mastered one turns fluidly through each of the directions without effort, almost magically.

Fair Lady Works
at Shuttles

It is important that sometime in a man's life he get to know a place, become bound up in a special piece of geography. Such a place need not be vast, exotic, brutally wild. It need only be a place that increases him, nourishes him.

Harry Middleton

Jodi turns her left foot in puts her right toe behind and spins around to face the next direction. Suddenly there is Sultan Mountain! We live on the other side of that compelling white triangle. In photo #6, in winter, we see Sultan's face directly above Silverton – scoured and shaped by the glacier. On this southern side of Sultan there were no glaciers so it's an easy walk up on alpine tundra, now covered with the first snowfall of the coming winter.

The Kogi tribe of northern Columbia consider their place to be a vast loom into which all the beings are woven. The earth itself is an immense loom on which the sun weaves the Fabric of Life. Solstices and Equinoxes provide the four directional corner posts of the loom. "Spiraling back and forth, the sun weaves day and night...light and darkness, life and death." The sun also weaves on the smaller loom of their own place, the Sierra Nevada mountains. It weaves between the four main ceremonial centers and includes all the beings of their place – human and non-human.

Form 70 – Fair Lady Works at Shuttles (2). The chi energy circulates throughout the turning body and is further increased by the raising and lowering of the hands.

" Nature's poems carved on tablets of stones, the simplest and most emphatic of her glacial compositions...[We] thus contemplate Nature's methods of landscape creation, and read the records she has carved on the rocks. "

John Muir

Jodi steps out, turns to the third direction and is immersed in the golden leaves of aspen. The bedrock under her feet is Precambrian (1.5 billion years ago) metamorphosed sediments – limestone recrystallized into marble. It has been polished by the moving glacier of long ago. It's beautiful rock and the polished surface feels smooth and sensuous as her feet move over it – the perfect rock for the spins and turns of Fair Lady. In some places there are parallel scratches, etched by the huge stones carried along in the sole of the glacier.

Rare wild plants grow in crevices, protected by the ancient rock and nourished by the falling aspen leaves which give nitrogen to the soil.

While turning to the four directions, breathing into the tan tien, Jodi is absorbed into the intimate ecology of four different ecosystems. No one has explained the depths of ecology as clearly as Edith Cobb, back in 1977, when she wrote: "In ecology we have for the first time in the history of thought, an instrument for the study of reciprocity and mutuality among categories of thought, as well as among divisions and levels in nature... . It permits us to evaluate reciprocal relations of living organisms with their total environment and with one another as living interdependent systems. This reciprocity...extends into a counterpoint between universe and geographical place. Plants, animals, and humans must now be thought of as living in ecosystems, in a web of related, interacting, dynamic energy systems."

Form 71 – Fair Lady Works at Shuttles (3).

Among the hills, what have I?
Along the ridges, white clouds lie,
Drifting purely for my felicity
– No man can trap them for your Majesty.
T'an Hung-ching

Jodi puts her right toe behind her, spins round on her left foot and faces down valley – down to where the Animas River flows out through the cleft, carrying water to all below: cities, fields, and orchards. The new snow on the higher peaks brings the promise of water for next spring. Jodi is turning through both space and time in Fair Lady.

The kind of understanding which comes from doing Fair Lady is much deeper than the "delimitation and exclusive differentiation of rational thinking", which is the usual human method of thinking. "But in nature," as David Hall tells us, "there can be no dominant principle defining any single order from which rational understanding might begin. The appropriation of the nature of things in terms of the mutual interfusion of each with all cannot result in traditional knowledge."

This special kind of knowledge is usually called mystical. But that's not the case. It's not ecstatic – the soul leaving and uniting with God – nor is it en-static as in some traditions, such as the Hindu, "where the focus of the experience is the soul itself."

"Nature-mysticism is distinguished from the other two forms since it focuses upon neither ecstasy nor en-stasy, but on an experience of the togetherness of all things which we may descibe as 'con-stasy' - that is to say, a 'standing with'. It is a sense of the presence of all things standing together in a felt unity. It is not merely the sense of being one with Nature… . It is the experience of the interfusion of each with each, the sense of compresence."

It's not differentiation but relatedness. The "totality" is literally completed by the rock Jodi is turning on, the flowers, the falling leaves. "We stress 'Where there is a will there is a way,' indicating that through sheer determination we can devise a means to a given end. The Taoist would reply that where there is a will, it and 'the Way' are surely not in harmony."

Form 72 – Fair Lady Works at Shuttles (4).

> **" The afternoon sun of autumn
> pours in its level light ... "**

Jodi moves backward, drawn ever deeper into the golden aspen.

In his "Process and Anarchy: A Taoist Vision of Creativity", the philosopher, David Hall tells us that "In classical China, the arts included much more than the traditional painting, poetry, music, and so on. Perhaps the most provocative and best-known art form deriving from classical China would likely not be termed an art form at all by those who encounter it for the first time. I refer to *Tai Chi Ch'uan* which is at one and the same time a meditative exercise, a technique for the maintenance of health and long life, a dance, and a system of self-defense. Above all, it is the single most direct and authentic expression of creativity as I have been discussing it... . The way of nonassetiveness seeks a harmony with Nature as becoming and thus eschews motivations toward control, progress, and domination of nature."

Form 81 – Step Back and Repulse Monkey (Right).

> ## *The golden gleam of aspen*
> ## *slanting through the forest*

Jodi's right hand is beginning to move into the push out motion of the palm, generating chi energy from the extension of the wrist tendon.

" 'Salvation' in the Taoist context," N. J. Girardot explains, "is more a matter of the healing of man in the fullness of cosmic life than it is a saving from the world. The implication seems to be that if a man can truly learn to reexperience *his* time as the primordial rhythm of Cosmic Time there will be a therapeutic effect bringing health, longevity, freedom and wisdom. The result of the return to the beginnings is a physical and spiritual wholeness but not an escape into a condition of absolute transcendental perfection."

Form 81 – Step Back and Repulse Monkey (Left).

Step Back and
Repulse Monkey

Autumn deepens...
a cool breeze
gently stirs the leaves.

Jodi's hands are just beginning to move into the final Repulse Monkey movement.

Somehow Tai Chi affords us humans the unique opportunity of fully experiencing our individual human nature while taking part in the abundance of all of surrounding nature. In terms of Western logic this can't happen, of course, but it can if we think in terms of Chuang Tzu's goal of repossessing "man's true nature," which is a way of *seeing* "that can come into play only when the distinction betwen 'inside' and 'outside,' between 'self' and 'things', between 'this' and 'that' has been entirely obliterated."

Form 81 – Step Back and Repulse Monkey (Right).

"Feet sinking into the yielding
leaves, rotting wood
Trees becoming earth,
Earth becoming trees
Forest rising from the abundance of its dying."

Jodi moves through the abundance of falling leaves. Through the trees, we see the fast moving water of Lime Creek, replenished by the newly fallen snow from high above.

Both the living and decaying processes in a forest lead to more life. "One of the roles of the growing organisms is to build structure, while one of the roles of the decaying organisms is to break down structure. Both phases are essential to the ecological processes that have evolved in forests. These processes include the life cycles of vertebrates and invertebrates, fungi and bacteria, and the strategies used by plant structures to accumulate nutrients." (Victoria Stevens).

Form 85 – Brush Knee and Twist Step.

In China there is K'uei who alone held the power of harmony and whose drumming, tactile in its purpose, touched the musical stone that caused a hundred animals to dance and regulated rivers maintaining nature's syntax.... . His drum beat was the voice of celestial time, rhythm and motion and as the musician to the great Yu brought about the step of Yu within the sky: a micromegaral translation from local earth to vast sky in the pattern of the Dipper.

An Chinese Legend

Jodi Steps Up to Form Seven Stars. Her hands, held before her eyes, form the Chinese ideogram for seven as she looks to the sky. Seven Stars is the Dipper pointing toward the North Star. This Pole Star remains stationary while all the constellations revolve around it.

The Chinese felt that not only the entire natural universe revolved around the Pole Star, but human culture as well, and thus the Four Seasons proceed on their course.

Form 101 – Step Up to Form Seven Stars.

> *At the end of their year there is a special ceremony that an African tribe performs. At a given moment, the chanting and the drumming ceased…. For a few seconds absolute silence reigned. Then the drums broke out again in triumph as the gods invisibly returned with the new year in their arms.*
>
> P. L. Travers

In this photo the Pole Star is shown with the constellations revolving around it. This photo was taken by Randy Pietz from his house just above Silverton. We superimiposed it over a photo of Jodi doing Seven Stars.

There's a sudden ceasing of all motion, unique in Tai Chi, as Jodi Steps Up to Form Seven Stars. For a moment all is motionless. Then there's a very slow movement of the right fist down the left arm. Both hands are lowered, chest high, palms facing the earth, followed by a 360 degree, horizontal "lotus" kick. Thus through Tai Chi the world begins again.

Form 101 – Step Up to Form Seven Stars.

" Charged with leaves of gold...
Deep, deep lies the pure abyss... "
Bill Ruddy

Immediately after completing the "lotus" kick, Jodi raises her arms in the form, Shoot Tiger with Bow. The electric air of autumn and the smooth rock beneath her feet contribute to the chi energy built up in her body by this form. Chi energy continues to build as the last series of punches are completed - leading to the final Conclusion of Tai Chi.

Form 104 – Shoot Tiger with Bow.

Shoot Tiger with Bow

*"How near to good is wild!…Here is this vast, savage, howling mother of ours, Nature, lying all around, with such beauty and affection for her children. Give me a wildness whose glance no civilization can endure… .
So we saunter towards the Holy Land, till one day the sun shall shine more brightly than he has done, shall perchance shine into our minds and hearts, and light up our whole lives with a great awakening light, as warm and serene and golden as on the bankside in autumn."*

Henry David Thoreau

Form 108 – Embrace Tiger, Return to Mountain. In this opening movement of the Conclusion of Tai Chi, Jodi reaches high to gather in the chi energy above and below.

Embrace Tiger, Return to Mountai

"Golden leaves
drifting on the wind
sift on my sleeve"

Jodi finishes gathering all the chi energy around her, raises it to heart level in her cupped hands and then turning her hands over gently moves them down like falling leaves to her *tan tien*. At the same time, very slowly, she straightens her legs until she is standing erect.

Gazing out at the mountains before her, rooted to the rock, waterfall behind her, the end of autumn and the Conclusion of Tai Chi.

Form 108 – Conclusion of Grand Terminus.

At the end of the day, Jodi and I turn to look at Bear Mountain. Back in the springtime we did Tai Chi near the gushing water and Bear Mountain was above us. Now it is autumn, with early snow and we are on the opposite side of the mountain with Silverton lying just over the mountain...

return to mountain

Tai chi

between heaven and eart

In Addendum

Because the original sources to which I refer in this manuscript use the older system of Wade-Giles romanization, I follow that usage.

Romanization is a system to transform Chinese characters into an alphabetical system. The older Wade-Giles system was based on the French language. At that time French was the language which everybody used – not only intellectuals, but the upper classes of most European countries including Russia. The word "Peking," when pronounced the French way, is much closer to the original Chinese "Beijing" than is the newer Pinyin system. The Pinyin system of romanization is based on the English language and thus requires the use of all the x's and q's, making it most unwieldy.

Please note the structuring of the reference notes is based on that of Barabara Tuchman's form. Barbara was the author of *Guns of August*, which is on the list of the 100 best non-fiction books of the twentieth century.

Reference Notes

I have made these Reference Notes easy for the general reader to use as well as provided all the information necessary for academic use.

For a particular entry in the Reference Notes, I first list the page in the main text where the quotation appears. Next, the opening words of the material I am quoting are listed within quotation marks. This is followed by the author's name in boldface, while the rest of the listing is in regular type. Further information is provided after the words in boldface, **Add. Notes:**

If I feel that a particular subject needs further documentation, I list that subject in small capitals at the beginning of the listing.

I list the most authentic sources whenever possible.

Part One

Chapter 1 Tai Chi

p. 15   Supreme Ultimate: See **Joseph Needham**, *Science and Civilization in China* vol. 2. Cambridge: Cambridge University Press,1956, p. 464 ff. **Add Notes:** The first volume of this definitive work came out in 1954. Recently, Needham wrote: "The work will be complete in some 25 volumes." Needham is the world's foremost scholar on the interaction of Chinese science and culture.

p. 15   Substance and Relationship: See **E. R. Hughes**, *The Great Learning and the Mean-in-Action.* New York: Dutton, 1943, p. 52.

p. 16   "essentially your ecosystem...": **Gregory Bateson**, Alfred Korzybski Memorial Lecture 1970." *General Semantics Bulletin*, Vol. 37 (1970), pp. 5–13.

p. 16   "across the pathways...": **Gregory Bateson**, "Pathologies of Epistemology." Second Conference on Mental Health in Asia and the Pacific, 1969. Hawaii: East-West Center Press, 1972. **Add Notes:** Both of these articles are reprinted in **Gregory Bateson**, *Steps To An Ecology of Mind.* New York: Ballantine Books Inc., 1972. p. 4 "the intercourse between Heaven...": **Laszlo Legeza**, *Tao Magic: The Chinese Art of the Occult.* New York: Pantheon Books, 1975, p. 70, Plate 48. p. 4 Wave Hands Like Clouds: Ibid: p. 70., Plate 42.

p. 17   "finally attained the supreme...": **Wen-Shan Huang**, *Fundamentals of Tai Chi Ch'uan: An Exposition of Its History, Philosophy, Technique, Practice and Application.* Hong Kong, South Sky Book Co., 1973, pp. 40 to 44. **Add Notes:** Wen-Shan Huang is a Professor at the Institute of Chinese Culture and Dean of the Faculty of Liberal Arts at Chu Hai College in Hong Kong. Also see Anna Seidel, "A Taoist Immortal of the Ming Dynasy:

Chang San-Feng." In Wm. Theodore de Bary, *Self and Society in Ming Thought.* New York: Columbia University Press, pp. 483-516.

Chapter 2 Seasonal Wheel of the Year

p. 21   "Heaven and earth...": **Ansho Togawa.** Quoted in H. Byron Earhart, "Four Ritual Periods of Haguro Shugendo in Northeast Japan." *History of Religions Journal*, Vol. 5, No. 1, pp. 93–113.

p. 21   "With the heaven and earth...": **Kuang-Ming Wu**, *The Butterfly as Companion: Meditations on the First Three Chapters of the Chuang Tzu.* Albany: State University of New York Press, 1990, p. 17.

p. 21   "The sound comes...": **Kuang-Ming Wu**, *Chuang Tzu: World Philosopher at Play.* Atlanta: Scholars Press, 1982, p. 79.

p. 21   "the words, the reader...": Ibid, p. 34.

p. 21   "joint process by which...": **Albert Hofstadter**, "Introduction". In *Martin Heidegger, Poetry, Language, Thought.* p. xxi. Add. Notes: Hofstadter is the translator of this volume.

p. 22   "A number of other...": **Keith Basso**, *Wisdom Sits in Places.* Albuquerque: University of New Mexico Press, p. 64.

p. 22   "The native American...": **N. Scott Momaday**, "Native American Attitudes to the Environment." In Walter Holden Capps, Ed. *Seeing with a Native Eye.* New York, Harper, 1976, pp. 79-85.

p. 22   "The machine is adapted...": **Jerry Mander**, "Industrial Logic". *Resurgence,* No. 186, Jan/Feb. 1998, pp. 9-11.

p. 22   "I never say the earth...": **Lynn Margulis**, "Living by Gaia". In Jonathan White, Ed., *Talking on the Water: Conversations About Nature and Creativity.* San Francisco: Sierra Club, 1994, pp. 58-77.

Part Two

Winter

Intro: Yin and Yang: **Mai-Mai Sze**, *The Theory of Painting: A Study of the Ritual Disposition of Chinese Painting.* New York: Pantheon Books, 1956.

p. 26   "In this way the yin...": **Tung Chung-shu**. Quoted in D. Bodde, "Harmony and Conflict in Chinese Philosophy." In A. F. Wright, Ed., *Studies in Chinese Thought.* Chicago: University of Chicago Press, 1953.

p. 28   "Snow opens...": **Robert MacLean**, *Heartwood.* Silverton CO: Way of the Mountain, 1985, unpaged.

p. 28   "He does not indulge...": **Kuang-Ming Wu**, *Chuang Tzu: World Philosopher at Play.* Atlanta: Scholar's Press, 1982, p. 21.

p. 30   "The aesthetic of fresh snow...": **Lito Tejada-Flores**, "Introduction". In Peter Shelton, *Aspen Skiing: The First Fifty Years.* Telluride: Western Eye Press, 1997.

p. 30   "self-arrangment among...": **Kuang-Ming Wu**, *The Butterfly as Companion.* Albany: State University of New York Press, 1990, p. 172.

p. 34   "We feel our way..." Ibid., p. 314.

p. 34   Grand Turk: **Allen Nossaman**, *Many More Mountains*, Vol. 1 of *Silverton's Roots*. Denver: Sundance Publications Ltd., 1989, p. 152.

p. 36   "Great one!…": **Alice Fletcher** and **Francis LaFlesche**, "The Omaha Tribe." Bureau of American Ethnology, *Twenty-seventh Annual Report* (1911).

p. 36   "Embrace Tiger, Return to Mountain…" **Al Chung-liang Huang**, *Embrace Tiger, Return to Mountain: The Essence of Tai Chi*. Moab, Utah: Real People Press, 1973. pp 184 and 185. Reprinted 1998 by Celestial Arts, Berkeley, Ca.

p. 36   Return to Mountain: In China mountains have always been an important aspect of the culture. In their physical height and grandeur they seem to be between heaven and earth – not of this earth but halfway to heaven. The Chinese felt that a mountain was the center of the universe; or a pathway to heaven; or an abode of the gods.

    The K'un-lun mountains were often mentioned in Taoist classics and among early Tai Chi masters. They lie north and west of Han China. In reply to my query about why the K'un-lun mountains are so revered, I received a letter from Edwin Bernbaum explaining: "There are several reasons for this: first, the K'un-lun is the actual source of the Yellow River, second, the K'un-lun lies to the west of Han China, the direction Lao-tse headed after dictating the Tao-te-ching; third, the western region where it lies is one of the major regions associated with barbarians in Chinese thought; and fourth, that's where it was placed in the 2nd century BCE when the Silk Route was opened by a minister of the Chinese emperor who was seeking the Palace of the Immortals."

    Bernbaum is the author of the classic, *Sacred Mountains of the World*, published by the Sierra Club in 1990.

    The K'un-lun mountains were snow covered and to the travelers far below on the dusty Takla Makan Desert they truly seemed to be sacred.

    For more than two thousand years the Chinese have revered five peaks as the principal sacred mountains of China: T'ai Shan in the east, Heng Shan in the north, Hua Shan in the West, another Heng Shan to the south and Sung Shan in the center. There are also 4 other sacred mountains for the Buddhists in China. The word, Shan means mountain. Also see Chapter 3 of my book, *Earth Wisdom*.

p. 36   "movement and stillness…": **Huang**, *Embrace Tiger, Return to Mountain*. p. 185.

Spring

p. 40   Positive and Negative Ions: **Dolores LaChapelle**, *Earth Wisdom*. Silverton Co: Finn Hill Arts, 1984.

p. 40   Air Ions: **Richard Leviton**, "How the Weather Affects Your Health". *East West Journal*, Sept. 1989, 65–68.

p. 42   "Serotonin irritation syndrome…": **Albert P. Krueger** and **Ed. J. Reed**, "Biological Impact of Small Air Ions." *Science*, Vol. 193, pp. 1209–1213. **Add Notes:** Kreuger is a research bacteriologist at the Naval Biosciences Laboratory, School of Public Health, University of California, Berkeley.

    It is important to realize that the words, negative and positive, referring to ions, have to do with the electrical charge of plus or minus, not with the effects on the human being.

Negative electrical charges have good effects on humans; while positive charges, in general, have ill effects. This involves the brain chemical serotonin, which is a very powerful and versatile neurohormone. "For example it is capable of inducing profound neurovascular, endocrinal, and metabolic effects throughout the body." Referring to Olivereau's work: "He concluded that air ion-induced alterations in blood levels of serotonin account for very significant physiological changes in the endocrine glands and central nervous system. These, in turn, substantially alter basic physiological processes."

"Seventy years ago, Czermak found that 'common characteristics of certain weather fronts, such as the foehn, was the development of abnormally high concentrations of positive ions.' He thought that this might be the cause of illness in weather-sensitive people." The authors explain that "the sequence is: elevated density of positive ions, increased production of serotonin in the exposed subject, resultant evolution of the clinical syndrome, and rise in renal excretion of serotonin." The disease is successfully treated by inhalation of air containing large numbers of negative ions or by administration of serotonin-blocking drugs.

The authors state: "The current growth of world population and industrial activities function to produce large-scale atmospheric pollution, and the combination of air pollutants with positive ions is very dangerous to health."

p. 42 Mind: See **Gregory Bateson**, "Pathologies of Epistemology". Second Conference on Mental Health in Asia and the Pacific, 1969. Hawaii: East-West Center Press, 1972.

p. 44 "...stir like icicles...": **Robert MacLean**, "Joyeux Noel". In *Selected Poems* Lewisville, Pa: Outland Press, 1977, p. 48.

p. 44 See p. 44, second para. "A large part of Balinese...": **Gregory Bateson**, *Sacred Unity: Further Steps to an Ecology of Mind,* New York: Harper Collins, 1991, p. 87. **Add. Notes:** In a recent book (1995) on Gregory Bateson's work, the author states: "One such writer, Dolores LaChapelle, has found a happy combination of metaphor and literality and action in her Way of the Mountain Center at Silverton, Colorado, by promoting rituals of connectedness through climbing, skiing and Tai Chi." Quoted in Peter Harries-Jones, *A Recursive Vision, Ecological Understanding and Gregory Bateson.* Toronto: University of Toronto Press, 1995, pp. 214-215.

p. 44 "kinesthetic socialization...": **Gregory Bateson**, Ibid., p. 85.

p. 44 "heaven at peace...,": **T. Y. Pang**, *On Tai Chi Chuan.* Bellingham, Washington: Azalea Press, 1987, p. 93.

p. 46 "The land speaks to us...": **Judyth Hill**, "The Last Story". In *A Presence of Angels.* Santa Fe: Sherman Ashe Publishing, 1995, p. 61.

p. 46 "move sedately...": *Field Guide to the Birds of North America.* National Geographic Society, 1987, p. 54

p. 48 "Mountains loom...": **Tahirussawichi**, Pawnee leader of the Hako Ceremony. Recorded by **Alice Fletcher**, *Bureau of American Ethnology, Twenty-second Annual Report*, Pt. 2 (1904). **Add Notes:** The basic Pawnee name for the ceremony is *Ruktaraiwarius*, meaning "stick of wood, shaking and moving" – the wands carried in the ceremony. The Omaha tribe's name is Hako, derived from *hakkow*, "breathing mouth of wood." for the same wands. Fletcher witnessed the ceremony among the Omaha in the early 1880's. The Omahas, Ponkas and Dakota told her that the Pawnee still preserved it in its entirety. In 1898 she saw the ceremony among the Pawnee and then did four years of work on it. Tahirussawichi was 70 years old when she worked with him.

p. 48   "Chinese thought refused to separate...": **Joseph Needham**, *Science and Civilization in China* vol. 2. Cambridge: Cambridge University Press, 1956, p. 270.

p. 48   The Powers: **Alice Fletcher**, Bur. of Amer. Ethnology, (1904). **Add. Notes:** Sir James Fraser in his classic, *The Golden Bough*, (12 volumes 1890 to 1915) found the key words to be "powers superior to man" – The powers as being more encompassing than gods.

p. 48   "Higher Powers...": **Vine Deloria**, "Sacred Lands and Religious Freedom". In *Native American Rights Fund, Legal Review,* v. 16, No. 2 Summer 1991, pp l–3. **Add. Notes:** Among the northern Sioux (Dakota), the words, *Wakan Tanka* mean "the Great Mystery", according to Ake Hultkrantz, "The Concept of the Supernatural in Primal Religion." *History of Religions Journal*, Feb. 1983, v. 22 No.3. *Wakan Tanka* does not mean the Great Spirit. Most Amerindians did not have a single great spirit. This concept was forced on them by Christian missionaries.

p. 48   Engineer Mountain named by Ruffner: **Allen Nossaman**, *Many More Mountains*, vol. l Silverton's Roots. Denver: Sundance Publications, 1989, pp. 140–141.

p. 48   Geology of Engineer Mountain: **Rob Blair**, *The Western San Juan Mountains*, Niwot Colorado: University Press of Colorado, 1996, p. 268–269.

p. 50   "A thing is right...": **Aldo Leopold**, *A Sand County Almanac.* London: Oxford University Press, 1966, pp. 224–225.

p. 50   "Flow down...": **Al Chung-liang Huang**, "Return to Inner Mountain." In Michael Tobias and Harold Drasdo, eds. *The Mountain Spirit.* Woodstock, New York: The Overlook Press, 1979. pp. 143–144.

p. 52   "In the gift of the outpouring...": **Martin Heidegger**, "The Thing." In *Poetry, Language, Thought.* New York: Harper Colophon Books, 1975, p. 173.

p. 52   "Opening of the Peak Ceremony": **H. Byron Earhart**, "Four Ritual Periods of Haguro Shugendo in Northeast Japan". *History of Religions* Journal Vol. 5 No. 1, pp. 93–113.

p. 54   "The fecund Spring...": **Kenneth Rexroth**, trans. *Love and the Turning Year: One Hundred More Poems from the Chinese.* New York: New Directions, 1970, p. 8.

p. 54   "superior but not immortal...": **Fosco Maraini**, *Meeting with Japan.* New York: Viking Press, 1960, pp. 144–146.

p. 56   Mother Mountain: **Vincent Scully**, *The Earth, The Temple and the Gods: Greek Sacred Architecture.* New York: Frederick A. Praeger, Publishers, 1969, pp. 80–84. First published by Yale University Press in 1962.

p. 56   Vagina of the Earth: **Paul Shepard**, "The Cross Valley Syndrome." *Landscape*, spring 1961, p. 4-8. **Add. Notes:** Shepard asks "How are we to explain this recurrent vision, and the elation of travelers, tourists and artists when confronted with this type of scenery? One answer…is to be found in our deep-seated, if unconscious, tendency to liken earth forms to human forms… . The prevalence of the primordial image of the earth-mother is a familiar instance." The passages of the body have long been recognized by anthropologists as having special significance in primitive orientation.

     Quoting Mircea Eliade, Shepard states: "If the earth is thought of as a living fecund mother...all that she produces is both organic and animated… . Mines, like the mouths of rivers have been likened to the matrix of the earth mother." The word *bi* in Egyptian is translated as vagina or shaft of a mine. The same symbol can be applied to grottoes and caves and narrow canyons. Even though we might consciously not notice this symbolism; at an unconscious level we still do. Quoting Eliade again, we have this "cosmic relationship to the environment." Shepard continues: "One might say that at a remote period man was less aware of belonging to the human species than of a cosmo-biological participation in the life of his surroundings…. This sort of experience established a mystic solidarity with the place, the intensity of which extends to our day in popular traditions and in folklore."

p. 56   "are disclosed as power…": **Vincent Vycinas**, *Search for Gods*. The Hague: Martinus Nijhoff, 1972.

p. 56   "Let us play our lives…": **Wu**, *Chuang Tzu*. Opening dedication, no page number.

p. 58   "every needle thrilling…": **John Muir**, *The Mountains of California*.

p. 58   "one of the very curious…" **Bateson**, *Sacred Unity*, p. 267.

p. 60   "The life…": **Jaime de Angulo**. Quoted in Bob Callahan, A Jaime de Angulo Reader. Berkeley: Turtle Island Press, 1979, p. xii.

p. 62   "The wild…": **Alan Drengson**, "Wild Journeyings" manuscript. **Add Notes:** Drengson is the publisher and editor of *The Trumpeter: Journal of Ecosophy*. He is a philosophy professor at the University of Victoria in Victoria Canada.

p. 62   "the binding and interconnecting…": **Elaine Jahner**, "The Spiritual Landscape."abola , Vol. 2 No. 3.

p. 64   "The Spirit of Restoration…": **Freeman House**, "Shasta Bioregional Gathering." San Francisco, Planet Drum, 1997.

p. 64   Cutler Formation: **Donald L. Baars**, The Colorado Plateau: A Geologic History Albuquerque: University of New Mexico Press, 1991, pp. 152–153.

p. 66   "In breathing one…": **Joseph Needham**, *Sci. & Civil.* Vol. 2, pp 143–144.

Summer

p. 69   "The Perfect Emperor…": **N. J. Girardot**, *Myth and Meaning in Early Taoism*. Berkeley: University of California Press, 1983, p. 30.

p. 69   "to protect from…": **E. O. James**, *Seasonal Feasts and Festivals*. London: Barnes & Noble, 196. **Add. Notes:** James was Professor Emeritus of the History of Religion at the University of London and Fellow of King's College, London, with a lifetime's study of religion.

p. 69   "The magic and ritual…": **Girardot**, *Myth and Meaning*, p. 182.

p. 70   "Tai Chi on the mountain's flank…": **Michael Adams**, "Broken Hand Peak". In *Broken Hand*. Golden CO: Longhand Press, 1991, p. 9. **Add. Notes:** For some years Rick Medrick and I did a workshop called Breaking Through. We did mountain climbing and river running and Tai Chi each morning. We taught the participants rock climbing unroped, Tai Chi style. Then we took them up to the high mountains of the Crestone range. On the way up Broken Hand Peak we did Tai Chi on a grassy flat spot at about 11,000 ft. elevation.

Mike Adams was one of our staff. Broken Hand Peak was named after an early fur trapper who lost three fingers in a trap. The Indians named him Broken Hand. Fitzpatrick was his name.

p. 70   Length of the Rio Grande River: **Michael Collier**, **R. Webb** and **John Schmidt**, *Dams* *and Rivers: Primer on the Downstream Effects of Dams.* Tucson: U.S. Geological Survey, 1996, p 29.

p. 70   Stony Pass: For a definitive history of the early days' travels through this pass see **Allen Nossaman**, *Many More Mountains*, Vol. 1 and 2. Denver: Sundance Publications, 1989 and 1993.

p. 72   "They are aware...": **Robert Payne**, *The White Pony*, New York: New American Library Edition, p. 24.

p. 72   Four Great Powers: Sword, an Oglala priest. Quoted in **J.R. Walker**, "The Sun Dance and other Ceremonies of the Oglala Division of the Teton Dakota". *Anthropological Papers of the American Museum of Natural History*, XVI,t II, New York, 1917.

p. 72   Tirawahat: **Von Del Chamberlain**, *When the Stars Come Down to Earth: Cosmology of the Skidi Pawnee Indians of North America.* Los Altos, CA: Ballena Press and College Park Maryland: Center for Archaeostronomy, University of Maryland, 1982, pp. 47–49. (A Cooperative Publication)

p. 72   Kailas: **Lama Govinda**, *The Way of the White Clouds.* Berkeley: Shambala, 1971, pp. 199-201. **Add. Notes:** Kailas (22,028 ft.) is in Tibet. It's 1500 miles between the mouth of the Indus River on the West and the mouth of the Brahmaputra on the East side of India. The width of the subcontinent of India is between them. The Brahmaputra River is 1680 miles long and the Indus River is about 1700 miles long.

p. 74   "Hither Winds, come...": **Fletcher**, *Bur. of Amer. Ethnology,* 1904,

p. 76   "To soar and to roam...": **Wu**, *The Butterfly*, p. 83.

p. 76   "Heat is given off...": **John Craighead, F. Craighead** and **Ray Davis**, *A Field Guide to Rocky Mountain Wildflowers.* Boston: Houghton Mifflin Co., 1963, p. 61.

p. 78   "I, however..." **F. Nietzsche**, "Thus Spoke Zarathustra: A Book for Everyone and No One." In R. J. Hollingdale, trans. *Ecce Homo.* New York: Penguin Books, 1979, pp. 107–108.

p. 80   "The experience of mountains...": **Harry Middleton**, *On the Spine of Time: A Flyfisher's Journey Among Mountain People, Streams and Trout.* Boulder: Pruett Publishing Co., 1997, p. 93.

p. 80   "In their non-human…": **George Santayana**. Quoted in William Everson, *Archetype West*, Berkeley: Oyez, 1976, pp. 57–59.

p. 82   "Verily, one alone…": **Fletcher** and **LaFlesche**, "The Omaha Tribe", pp. 570–572.

p. 82   "…a way of understanding…": **Arne Naess**, "Modesty and the Conquest of Mountains". In Michael Tobias and Harold Drasdo, eds. *The Mountain Spirit* New York: Overlook Press, 1979, pp. 13–16.

p. 82   The Great Mystery: **Ake Hultkrantz**, "The Concept of the Supernatural in Primal Religion". *History of Religions* Journal , Vol. 22, No. 3, Feb. 1983. **Add Notes:** The best translation of Wakan Tanka is The Great Mystery.

p. 82   "Inyan – the rocks...": **Lame Deer**, *Lame Deer Seeker of Visions: The Life of A Sioux Medicine Man.* New York: Simon and Schuster, 1972, pp. 113 and 275.

p. 82   "I was alone...": **Yuichiro Miura**, "The Great Ski Caper". (as told to Darrell Houston) Seattle Times, June 18, 1972.

p. 84   "Alongside the peaks...": **Alan Grad**, "Flying Mountains and Walkers of Emptiness: Toward a Definition of Sacred Space in Japanese Religion." *History of Religions* Journal. Vol. 20, No. 3 (Feb. 1982), pp. 195–221.

p. 84   Cloud Movement: **Laszlo Legeza**, *Tao Magic: The Chinese Art of the Occult*. London: Thames & Hudson, Ltd., 1975, p. 70 (Plate 42).

p. 84   "respond infinitely and freely...: **Toshihiko Izutsu**, *A Comparative Study of the Key Philosophical Concepts in Sufism and Taoism*. Tokyo: Institute of Cultural and Linguistic Studies, Keio University, Minatoku, 1967, pp. 46 and 51.

p. 86   "The hills waver...": **Robert MacLean**, "Beginning to Meditate", p. 5.

p. 86   "A long time...": **Grad**, "Flying Mountains."

p. 86   "Clouds in the stratus...": **Vincent Schaefer** and **J. Day**, *A Field Guide to the Atmosphere*. Boston, Houghton Mifflin, 1981, p. 52.

p. 88   "To drift like Clouds...": Quoted by **Gary Snyder** in *Earth House Hold*. New York: New Dimensions Books, 1969, p. 44.

p. 88   "does not remember..."; **Wu**, *The Butterfly*, p. 80 and 81.

p. 90   "Heaven and earth...": **Ansho Togawa**. Quoted in Earhart, "Four Periods of Haguro Shugendo." **Add. Notes:** Ansho's "knowledge of the doctrine and practice of *Haguro yamabushi* is unrivaled."

p. 90   Austronesian cultural sources: **Girardot**, *Myth and Meaning*. p. 170. **Add. Notes:** Girardot refers to "the work of several scholars who point to the general linguistic and cultural significance of the so-called Austroasiatic and Austronesian (Mayalo-Polynesian) traditions" and to "the role of various local tribal traditions in the ancient cultural areas of South China, Indo-China, and insular southeast Asia."

p. 90   Nu-kua, serpent goddess: **Girardot**, *Myth and Meaning,* p. 202–206.

p. 90   "linked with the legendary...": Ibid., p. 203.

p. 90   "transformation of the continuous...": Ibid., p. 204.

p. 90   "Once we have...": **Freeman House**, "Remembering the Instruction of the Land." *Raise the Stakes*, No. 27. Planet Drum, Publisher.

p. 92   "The Blue Dragon.,..": **Richard Wilhelm**, trans. *The Secret of the Golden Flower.* New York: Harcourt Brace & World, 1962. p. 62.

p. 92   Tan Tien: **V Hunt**, "A Study of Structural Integration from Neuromuscular, Energy field and Emotional Approaches." Boulder: Rolf Institute for Structural Integration. Add. Notes: In Kristofer Schipper's work, he states: "The important term, tan-t'ien appears for the first time in the original Huang-t'ing ching, translated as Book of the Yellow Court...The original tan-t'ien is a spot in the belly, traditionally situated 'under' the navel." Schipper continues: "As a matter of fact, there is only one definite identification of the tan-t'ien, 'the lower tan-t'ien is the root of human life...At three inches below the navel.' This definition is in the Jade Calendar Book which is part of "The seven oracles of the cloudy book case", which is a Taoist encyclopedia of the eleventh century. Schipper sums up: "It is clear that the real Alchemical Field is in the belly. It is there where everything takes place." Kristofer Schipper, "The Taoist Body". *History of Religions* Journal, Vol. 17, No. 3, pp. 355–386. Schipper is Dutch but he studied Taoism for some years in China and eventually became a Taoist priest.

p. 92   Gushing Spring: It is an acupuncture point "at the center of the foot where the root lies." **B. Pang Jeng Lo** and M. Inn, R. Amacker, and S. Foe. *The Essence of Tai Chi Chuang: The Literary Tradition*. North Atlantic Press, Richmond, CA,1979, p. 100.

p. 94   "Lao Tzu says...": **Izutsu**, *Comparative Study,* p. 134.

p. 94   "To come home...": **Wu**, *Chuang Tzu*, p. 115 & 116.

p. 94   "If I am under...": Ibid, p. 128.

p. 94   Coarse Woody Debris: **Victoria Stevens**, "The Ecological Role of Coarse Woody Debris." In Alan Drengson and Duncan Taylor, *Ecoforestry: The Art and Science of Sustainable Forest Use*. Gabriola Island Canada: New Society Publishers, 1997, pp. 89-101.

p. 96   Indian Paintbrush: **Craighead & Craighead**, *A Field Guide to Rocky Mountain Wildflowers*, p. 170.

p. 96   "every organism...": **Lynn Margulis**, In *Jonathan White, Talking on the Water*. San Francisco: Sierra Club Books, 1994, pp 57–77. Add. Notes: Lovelock first stated the Gaia Hypothesis in 1972. Writing about his friendship and collaboration with Lynn Margulis he states: "Lynn, from her wide knowledge and deep understanding of organisms – especially micro-organisms, put flesh on the bare bones of my physical chemistry." He talks about the 25 years since 1972 and how the hypothesis has been evolving and becoming clearer and sums up: "Now, it can be stated as the theory of an evolving system: a system made from the living organisms of the Earth and from their material environment, the two parts tightly coupled and indivisible. This evolutionary theory views the self-regulation of climate and chemical composition as emergent properties of the system." This is from an article by James Lovelock, "Travels with an Electron Capture Detector." *Resurgence* No. 187 March/April, 1998.

p. 98   "As children...": **Casey Walker**, Editor, *Wild Duck Review* (February 1997), p. 2.

p. 100 "Like a Taoist sage...": **John Briggs** and **F. David Peat**, *Turbulent Mirror: An Illustrated Guide to Chaos Theory and the Science of Wholeness*. New York: Harper and Row, 1990, p. 202-203.

p. 102 Use of Fists: The full name of Tai Chi is Tai Chi Ch'uan. Ch'uan means fist or boxing and is usually part of the title for all exercises based on the Martial Arts. This is explained in *Lo, Essence of Tai Chi*, p. 37.

p. 102 "Against this trend...": **Briggs** and **Peat**, *Turbulent Mirror*, p. 201.

p. 104 "A south wind...": **MacLean**, "Spring." In *Heartwood*.

p. 104 "You will meet beauty...": **Bateson**, *A Sacred Unity*, p. 311.

p. 104 "I believe...": : Ibid., p. 313.

p. 106 "wild energy of renewal...": **Middleton**, *Spine of Time*.

p. 106 "Nothing so moves the soul...,": **James Hillman**, In *Hillman and Ventura, We've Had a Hundred Years of Psychotherapy and the World's Getting Worse*. San Francisco, Harper, 1992, p. 130.

p. 108 "there's life here...": **J. Bryan**, "Earthville." Unpublished. Copyright 1998.

p. 108 "our culture...": **Hillman**, *Hundred Years of Psychotherapy*, pp. 126, 129 and 130.

p. 110 "as the seat...": **Richard Pilgrim**, "The artistic and the Religio-Aesthetic Tradition in Japan." *History of Religions* Journal , v. 17 No. 3, pp. 285–305.

p. 110 "It is a liberation...,": **Karlfied Durckheim**, *Hara: The Vital Center of Man*. London: Allen and Unwin, 1962, pp. 33, 37 and 56.

p. 110 "he who cherishes...": **Basho**, Oi no kobumi. Quoted in *Daisetzu Suzuki, Zen and Japanese Culture*. New York: Pantheon Books, 1959, p. 258.

p. 112 "Sun pulsating...": **MacLean**, "The Pond". In *Selected Poems*, p. 13.

p. 114 "chose its residence...": **Allan Grad**, "Flying Mountains".

p. 116 "He danced the moor...": **Jean Giono**, *Joy of Man's Desiring*. San Francisco, North Point Press, 1980, p. 103.

p. 116   "harmonize movement...": **Alan Drengson**, "Wild Journeying" manuscript.

p. 118   "In the Manyoshu...": **Joseph Kitagawa**, "A Past of Things Present: Notes on Major Motifs of Early Japanese Religion." *History of Religions* Journal, Vol. 20, No. 1 (August, 1980), pp. 27–33. **Add Notes:** The first part of the Manyoshu, dates back to the years 645–672.

p. 120   "I rest on the piled-up...": **Hsieh Ling-yun**. In Paul Z. Panish, trans. "Hsieh Ling-yun's Poetical Essay on My Mountain Dwelling", Degree in Master of Art in Oriental Language and Literature, University of California at Berkeley in December 1973.

p. 120   "Piping comes when...": **Wu**, *The Butterfly*, p. 240–241.

p. 122   "The rocks are ringing...": Piaute Ghost Dancer chant. In **James Mooney**, trans. "The Ghost Dance Religion." *Bur. of Amer. Etnol. Fourteenth Annual Report,* pt. 2 (1892–3).

p. 122   "This leads us...": **Wu**, *The Butterfly*, p. 242 and 246.

p. 124   "up high in the mountains...,": **Middleton**, *Spine of Time*, p. 24.

p. 124   "Music is piped...": **Wu**, *The Butterfly*, pp. 254–255.

p. 126   "A large part...": **Bateson**, *Sacred Unity*, p. 87.

p. 126   The Cock: **Siegfried Wichmann**, *Japonisme, Japanese Influence on Western Art in the 19th and 20th Centuries*. New York: k Lane (A Division of Crown Publishers), 1985, p.114.

p. 128   Legend of Emperor Yao: Ibid.

p. 130   "As the sun pours...": **Walkin' Jim Stolz**, "All Along the Great Divide." Song on the "Spirit Is Still on the Run" tape. Lone Coyote Records, Box 209, Big Sky, MT. 59716. Add. Notes: The two main sources for background on the ponderosa pine: Bob Blair, Managing Ed. *The Western San Juan Mountains: Their Geology, Ecology and Human History.* Niwot CO: University Press of Colorado. Audrey DeLella Benedict, *A Sierra Club Naturalist's Guide: The Southern Rockies.* San Francisco: Sierra Club, 1991, pp. 272–277.

p. 132   "The number three...": **Wu**, *The Butterfly* p. 318.

p. 132   "Vernadsky showed us...": **Lynn Margulis**, "Living by Gaia". In J. White, ed., *Talking on the Water,* pp. 57-77.

p. 134   "We are left in awe...": **George Nakashima**, *The Soul of a Tree*. Tokyo and San Francisco: Kodansha Int., 1981, p. 81.

p. 136   "I have noticed...": **Brave Buffalo**. Quoted in Francis Densmore, Bulletin 61 of the Bur. of Amer. Ethno., p. 208.

p. 138   "To fill the pattern...": **MacLean**, "Earthswimmer." In *Selected Poems*, p. 22.

p. 138   "Man's love for...": **Hugh Iltis**, "Flowers and Human Ecology." In Cyril Selmes, ed., New Movements in the Study of Biology and Teaching of Biology . London: Maurice Temple Smith, 1947.

p. 140   "Of all the pines...": **John Muir**. Quoted in *Benedict, A Sierra Club Naturalist's Guide: The Southern Rockies*, p. 272.

p. 140   "No one...": **Paul Shepard**, "The Wilderness is Where by Genome Lives". In *Traces of An Omnivore*. Washington D.C. and Covelo CA: Island Press, 19906, pp. 215–221. This essay was first printed in 1995 in *Whole Terrain, Reflective Environmental Practice*. Vol. 4 1995/96. Antioch New England Graduate School.

Autumn

p. 143 "Now, what of...": **Frederick Adams**, "Land, Sky, Love Temple," Feraferia Journal, (1969).

p. 143 "At no other time...": **Juliet Bredon** and **Igor Mitrophanow**, *The Moon Year*. Shanghai, Kelly and Walsh Ltd., 1927.

p. 144 "blazes, scattering...": **MacLean**, "The Birch". In *Selected Poems*, p. 29.

p. 146 "a mind obeying...": **Basho**. Quoted in William R. LaFleur, "Saigyo and the Value of Nature." *History of Religions*, Vol. 13, No. 3 (Feb. 1974), pp 227-248.

p. 148 "soars in majesty..." Manyoshu, ancient Japanese poem collection. Quoted in **Joseph Kitagawa**, " 'A Past of Things Present': Notes on Major Motifs of Early Japanese Religion", Vol. 20, No. 1, (August 1980).

p. 148 "Tao as the source...": **Girardot**, *Myth and Meaning*, p. 49.

p. 148 "Circular power...": **Bruce Wilshire**, *Wild Power, The Primal Roots of Modern Addiction*. New York and Oxford: Rowman and Littlefield Publishers Inc., 1998, p. 49.

p. 150 "making the spring...": **Chuang Tzu**. Quoted in Wu, *The Butterfly*, p. 17. **Add Notes:** Wu explains this phrase which occurs in one of the Outer Chapters of Chuang Tzu, Chapter 18, where Chuang Tzu talks of a dream connection with a roadside skull.

p. 150 "we had better...": **Chuang Tzu**, Chapter 3 titled "Nourishing Life – Its Inner Principle." Quoted in Wu, *The Butterfly*, p. 285.

p. 150 "all this is joy...": **Wu**, *The Butterfly*, p. 317.

p. 150 "unmistakably...": Ibid.

p. 150 "In sum...": Ibid, p. 19.

p. 152 "The image of...": Ibid. pp. 341 and 342.

p. 152 "These two qualities...": Ibid., p. 172.

p. 154 "Their breathing...": **Izutsu**, *Comparative Study of Tao and Sufi*, p. 165.

p. 154 "Through opening to...": **Wilshire**, *Wild Hunger*, p. 209.

p. 154 "The resemblance of this..." **Wu**, *The Butterfly*, p. 340.

p. 158 "lies in the middle...": **D. H. Lawrence**. Quoted in Rhys Davies, " D. H. Lawrence in Bandol." *Horizon II*, Oct. 1940, pp. 191–208. **Add. Notes:** "with his solar plexus", Cynthia Asquith in *Remember and Be Glad*. London, James Barrie, 1952, p. 144.

p. 158 "the mind from the tyranny..." **Fosco Maraini**, *Meeting with Japan*. New York: The Viking Press, 1960, pp 289–290.

p. 160 Chinese Honoring Horses: **H. G. Creel**, Chapter titled: "The Role of the Horse in Chinese History." In *What is Taoism and Other Studies in Chinese History*. Chicago: University of Chicago Press, 1970. Add. Notes: For the horsemen invaders see Paul Shepard, *The Others: How Animals Made Us Human*. Washington D.C./Covelo CA: Shearwater Books, 1996, pp. 243–244 and 250–255.

p. 162 "I am not afraid...": **Rachel Carson**. Quoted in John Elkington, "Mother to Millions". *Resurgence*, July/August 1998.

p. 164 Sacred Person Weaving: On the seventh day of the seventh month the "Weaver woman" our star, Vega, and the herd boy Altair meet. "Sacrificial offerings were made to the goddess, the heavenly weaver." Magpies or ravens made a bridge across the heavenly river, the Milky Way, so that the two could meet once a year. **W. Eberhard**, *The Local*

Cultures of South and East China. Leiden: E. J. Brill, 1968. **Add Notes:** "The character *ching* meant the warp set up on a loom. But after Confucius' time there came the practice of recording a teacher's noteworthy dicta, and these records came to be called *ching*, i.e., warp, teaching on which disciples could weave the woof of their ampliciations." **E. R. Hughes**, "Epistemological Methods in Chinese Philosophy." In Charles A. Moore, ed., *The Chinese Mind, Essentials of Chinese Philosophy and Culture*. Honolulu: East West Center Press, University of Hawaii Press, 1967. pp 77–103.

The Japanese weaver woman was Amaterasu. See **Alan L. Miller**, "The Heavenly Weaving Maiden: The Cosmic Weaver in Early Shinto Myth and Ritual." *History of Religions* Vol. 24 No. 1, Aug. 1984, pp. 27–47.

p. 164   "not a leap..." **Paul Shepard**, *Traces of An Omnivore*. Washington D.C./Covelo, CA Shearwater Books, 1996, p. 90.

p. 166   "It is important..." **Middleton**, *On the Spine of Time*, p. 92.

p. 166   "Spiraling back and forth...": **Gerardo Reichel-Dolmatoff**, "The Loom of Life: A Kogi Principle of Integration." *Journal of Latin America Lore*, No. 4, pp. 5–27.

p. 168   "Nature's poems carved...": **John Muir**, *The Mountains of California*, originally published in 1894.

p. 168   Precambrian: **Halka Chronic**, Roadside Geology of Colorado, Missoula, Montana: Mountain Press Publishing Co., 1980, p. 240–241.

p. 170   "In ecology...": **Edith Cobb**, *The Ecology of Imagination in Childhood*, New York: Columbia University Press, 1977, p. 24. Reprinted by Dallas: Spring Press in 1993.

p. 170   T'an Hung-ching, a court advisor in ancient China, who went back to the mountains on retirement. No other reference available.

p. 170   "delimitation and exclusive..." down to "we are surely not in harmony...": **David L. Hall**, "Process and Anarchy: A Taoist View of Creativity". *Philosophy East and West*, July 1978, pp. 270–284. **Add Notes:** Hall is a professor of Philosophy at the University of Texas at El Paso, Texas. The journal is published by the University Press of Hawaii.

p. 172   "In classical China...": Ibid. **Add Notes: Gregory Bateson**'s use of metaphor gives us still deeper insight into the importance of aesthetics. According to **Peter Harries-Jones**, "The parallel cases in Bateson's version of metaphor...evoke differing levels of sensuousness, which, in their combination, evoke the whole in human experience. The whole implicates primary process, vision, imagination, and the more abstract notions of aesthetics; the patterns of 'goodness,' symmetry, and beauty." Furthermore, Jones explains that: "Only when put into relation with each other do the objects juxtaposed in metaphor evoke meaning. They also evoke cumulative images of pattern. Unlike the rules of logic, which order a chain of reasoning in order to assert an identity, it is through metaphor and parables that we try to communicate truth." Then Jones quotes Bateson directly: "There is no other way. No 'literal' communication..." (This is from Bateson's "Notebooks" 29 Dec. 1976). The above material is from Jones, *A Recursive Vision, Ecological Understanding and Gregory Bateson,* p. 95. In Tai Chi the "cumulative images of pattern," underly all the forms.

p. 174   "Salvation is more...": **Girardot**, *Myth and Meaning*, p. 298.

p. 176   "that can come into...": **Arthur Waley**, *Three Ways of Thought in Ancient China*. Garden City: Doubleday, 1956, pp. 66 and 67

p. 178   "One of the roles...": **Stevens**, "The Ecological Role of Coarse Woody Debris."

p. 180   "In legendary China...": **Steve McCaffrey**, "Drum Language and the Sky Text". *Alcheringa Ethnopoetics,* Vol. 3 No. 1 (1977), pp. 78–84. **Add Notes:** My first Tai Chi teacher, Raymond Chung, told us that the position of the crossed fists makes the Chinese character for the number 7. There are seven stars in the Dipper and the two stars in the outer bowl of the cup point toward the North Star. The Pole Star, called Polaris, remains stationary while all the other stars move around it. Confucius said: "The North Star; it remains in place while all the other stars revolve in homage about it." (Analects , Ch. 2, paragraph 1). Quoted in **Herbert Fingarette**, *Confucius – The Secular as Sacred.* New York: Harper & Row, 1972, p 4.

     The Pawnee called the Pole Star, "the star that doesn't walk around." In **Chamberlain**, *When the Stars Came Down to Earth*, p. 106.

     The K'un-lun Mountains seem to be directly under the Pole Star. The famous Silk Route traversed the Takla Makan Desert just below these mountains.

     Just as the Pole Star is stationary while all turns around it, so our spine is stationary as we turn. The spine is our K'un-lun Mountain. In Tai Chi the spine is called the "Pivot of the Way", a Taoist term.

p. 182   "At the end of their year...": **P. L. Travers**, *What the Bee Knows* London: Penguin Books, 1993, p 86.

p. 184   "Charged with leaves of gold...": **Bill Ruddy**, unpublished ms.

p. 186   "How near to good...": **Henry David Thoreau**, "Walking." In *The Writings of Henry David Thoreau*. Riverside Edition, 1894.

p. 188   The number 8 is very important in Chinese culture. There are five elements: earth, wood, fire, water and metal. The interactions of Heaven, Earth, and Man create their culture. The reciprocal appropriation of the Five Elements and these three aspects of culture makes 8 – which refers to all of life. There is a magic Taoist diagram for this interaction, dating from the Tao-tsang, Taoist canon published under the Cheng-t'ung Emperor in 1436. The Taoist diagram is shown on p. 110 of Laszlo Legeza, *Tao Magic*: London, Thames and Hudson Ltd.,1975 and New York: Pantheon Books. Also see **Needham**, *Science and Civilisation in China,* Vol. 2, p. 461.

     There are 108 forms in the regular Yang form of Tai Chi. For this book, we took thousands of photographs and chose 80 of those which best illustrate human/nature reciprocal appropriation.

Selected Bibliography

Basso, Keith. *Wisdom Sits in Places*. Albuquerque: University of New Mexico Press, 1996.

Bateson, Gregory. *A Sacred Unity: Further Steps to an Ecology of Mind*. New York: Harper Collins, 1991.

_____. "Alfred Korzybski Memorial Lecture 1970." *General Semantics Bulletin* vol. 37 (1970):5-13.

_____. "Pathologies of Epistemology." Second Conference on Mental Health in Asia and the Pacific , 1969.

_____. *Steps to An Ecology of Mind*. New York: Ballantine Books Inc. 1972.

Bernbaum, Edwin. *Sacred Mountains of the World*. San Francisco: Sierra Club Books, 1990.

Blair, Rob. ed. *The Western San Juans: Their Geology, Ecology, and Human History*. Niwot:University Press of Colorado, 1996.

Briggs, John and F. David Peat, *Turbulent Mirror: An Illustrated Guide to Chaos Theory and the Science of Wholeness*. New York:Harper & Row, 1990.

Cobb, Edith. *The Ecology of Imagination in Childhood*. New York: Columbia University Press, 1977. Reprint Dallas: Spring Press, 1993.

Drengson, Alan and Duncan Taylor, eds. *Ecoforestry: The Art and Science of Sustainable Forest Use*. Gabriola Island, B.C. Canada: New Society Publishers, 1997.

_____. "Wild Journeyings". Unpublished manuscript, 1998.

Earhart, H. Byron. "Four Ritual Periods of Haguro Shugendo in Northeast Japan." *History of Religions* vol. 5 no l:93–113.

Fletcher, Alice. "The Hako: A Pawnee Ceremony." Bureau of American Ethnology, Twenty-second Annual Report. (1904).

_____, "The Omaha Tribe." Bureau of American Ethnology, Twenty-seventh Annual Report. Pt. 2 (1911).

Girardot, N. J. *Myth and Meaning in Early Taoism*. Berkeley: University of California Press, 1983.

Grapard, Alan. "Flying Mountains and Walkers of Emptiness: Toward a Definition of Sacred Space in Japanese Religion." *History of Religions* vol. 20, no. 3 (February 1982):195–221.

Hall, David L. "Process and Anarchy: A Taoist View of Creativity." *Philosophy East and West* (July 1978): 270–284.

Harries-Jones, Peter. *A Recursive Vision: Ecological Understanding and Gregory Bateson*. Toronto:University of Toronto Press, 1995.

Heidegger, Martin. *Poetry, Language, Thought*. New York: Harper & Row, 1975.

Hill, Judyth. *A Presence of Angels*. Santa Fe: Sherman Asher Publishing, 1995.

Hillman, James and M. Ventura. *We've Had a Hundred Years of Psychotherapy and the World's Getting Worse*. San Francisco: Harper, 1992.

Huang, Al Chung-liang. *Embrace Tiger, Return to Mountain: The Essence of Tai Chi*. Moab, Utah: Real People Press. 1973. Reprinted Berkeley: Celestial Arts, 1998.

_____. "Return to Inner Mountain," in *The Mountain Spirit*. Edited by Michael Tobias and Harold Drasdo. Woodstock: The Overlook Press, 1979.

Huang, Wen-Shan. *Fundamentals of Tai Chi Ch'uan: An Exposition of Its History, Philosophy, Technique, Practice and Application*. Hong Kong: South Sky Book Co., 1973.

Hultkrantz, Ake. "The Concept of the Supernatural in Primal Religion." *History of Religions* vol 22 no. 3 (February 1983).

Hughes, E. R. *The Great Learning and The Mean-in-Action*. New York: Dutton, 1943.

Izutsu, Toshihiko. *A Comparative Study of the Key Philosophical Concepts in Sufism and Taoism*. Tokyo: Keio University, 1967.

Kiragawa, Joseph. "A Past of Things Present:Notes on Major Motifs of Early Japanese Religion." *History of Religions* vol. 20, no. 1 (August 1980):27–33.